ALSO BY PATRICK NOBLE

Notes from the old Blair and Bush (2008)

Romantic Economics (2010)

The Commons of Soil (2011)

The Lost Coefficient of Time (2011)

A Potent Nostalgia (2013)

A Midsummer Night's Dream (2014)

Towards the Convivial Economy (2017)

Reclaiming Commons (2018)

WALKING HOME

PATRICK NOBLE

SMOKEHOUSE PRESS, Norwich

www.smokehousepress.co.uk

Published by Smokehouse Press, Norwich, 2020
www.smokehousepress.co.uk

Typeset in Cambria
by Smokehouse Press

Printed and bound in England by CMP

ISBN 978-1-9162832-1-3

Cover – 'The Weary Ploughman' by Samuel Palmer (begun in 1858)
– Courtesy of the Metropolitan Museum of Art, New York.

Dear Nicola,

I hope you enjoy the contents,

Patrick

With all my love to Becky, Huw, John and Owain,
who have made me proud
And to Tom – another member of our family
And to Pedro, who worked so well with us as I wrote this book.
And to Joyce, my love, my companion and my friend

CONTENTS

ILLUSTRATIONS

FOREWORD

These chapters have been written in sequence, each following and as part of the other, but, if my reader wishes to dip in, or skip a bit, then, I hope each chapter will stand well enough on its own.

The writing has been scented by events, contemporary to its clattering keyboard - between August 2019 and June 2020.

Yet, I hope it draws us from the ephemeral and back into deeper and slower passages of time.

I also hope that you can embark with pleasure and not as a chore and that my children and all our children can find a better landfall than some of those I suggest.

If we all walk home *beneath* the vapour trails, so that both work and pleasure end within walking distances from everyone's door, then such a landfall will be possible.

Last but not least, I'm honoured that Lawrence Woodward has put aside his other commitments to write the foreword to this book.. Like many of my fellow organic farmers and growers, we consider him the unwavering touchstone for truth, amid the prevailing, market-led perversion of original organic philosophy.

Patrick Noble, August 2020

INTRODUCTION

Patrick Noble is a formidable thinker and writer. He is clear-sighted and honest. He has vision and perspective, which may not be to everyone's taste but it is rooted in the experience of decades of living and working on the land, in a harmonious relationship with nature, within an area and its culture and therefore, it's a vision which cannot be ignored.

On the contrary, it demands attention because Patrick has worked hard at thinking through and testing these experiences and honing them into a body of work which is in part philosophical, in part a penetrating analysis, in part a political manifesto; and as a whole, a celebration of the rural, the artisanal, the natural, the independent but communal ecosystem he believes the human spirit thrives in.

His writing is built around working "towards a Convivial Economy". This economy and society defy labelling. If you want to find socialism there, you can; if you want to find Adam Smith's idea of "sweet commerce", it's there; so are elements of "the Green New Deal" and Wendell Berry's "agrarian values", but none of them in a manner which conforms to tick boxes. The shape, the form and the relationship of them to each other and the whole, are moulded in a way which is uniquely Noble.

Many of Berry's themes are shared by Patrick but how they are worked, drawn out and built on are very different. Patrick is a working farmer who thinks and writes, not a professional writer who has a farm. But the really important point, and difference, is that Patrick's thinking and writing and, from the beginning his farming, is driven by the urgent need to find real practical solutions to the social, economic, political and humanitarian crises caused by living on a planet of finite and diminishing resources, where the resources are running out, the planet is burning and where its inhabitants seem pathologically incapable of change.

This book is about change. It's about how change has to happen and how farming, food, health, local economies and culture have to be at the centre of that change. It is challenging – and not just to the mainstream – it challenges the shallow thinking, the clichés, the hidden agendas and careerism of much of the green and alternative movements.

But it is also uplifting, optimistic and readable. Ultimately, it makes you feel that the right kind of change is possible and that the convivial society and economy would be a good place to live in.

Lawrence Woodward, OBE

****

Lawrence Woodward *is a director and co-founder of Beyond GM and Whole Health Agriculture. Having been a founder and director of the Organic Research Centre (ORC) for 30 years, Lawrence advises and speaks about the principles and methods of organic agriculture to a wide range of organisations. In 2001 he was awarded an OBE. for services to organic farming.*

CHAPTER 1 – ENERGY

All life is busy – energetic – converting mass to energy and energy to mass. We note energy in the causes and effects of motion and in the growth of individual organisms. A continuous fermentation both within organisms and in soil and sea through which all terrestrial cycles must pass, breaks biomass into simple, original minerals (biomass nutrients) and gases. To a farmer, as fermentation accelerates, so does the growth of her crops. Receding, or increasing fermentation is plainly visible, week by week in the paling, or deepening green of foliage. The energy is plain. The mass is plain. The increasing mass of her animals, or indeed, her children, is a consequence of the increasing mass and energy of her plants, which in turn, are a consequence of the power (acceleration) of soil fermentation and photosynthesis. That deepening green of cereal blades indicates increasing speed and increasing energy. Yes. Time and velocity are also plain – we say slow-growing; fast-growing and we have impatient appetites, dependant on Winter stores.

Temperature is critical to energy/mass exchanges and to rules of good husbandry. Fermentation happens anyway if temperatures and moisture are right. If plants are not available to take up those minerals (as in a bare fallow, or planting delayed by bad weather), then they will escape to water-courses. The gas that escapes to the air, will not be returned by photosynthetic re-balancing, but will accumulate in the atmosphere, to the degree and duration of the ferment of that one fallow field. Subsequent crop yield from that field will be smaller, because soil biomass will be smaller. Lifeless minerals and gases will have increased, while biomass and bio-energy will have diminished. We could look at it in these terms – a tendency for lifelessness will have become larger than a tendency for life. Optimum husbandry success is for dying and living to remain in balance. Dying and living are both dynamic. Lifelessness and dying are not at all the same things. Minerals and gases are either a part of a tendency for life, or of a tendency for lifelessness. My husbandry can swing the balance one way or the other. Humanity as a whole is choosing to swing the balance towards a lifeless planet.

Those who'd burn energetic biomass for mere energy, gas and ashes are approved by the IPCC and most government departments as achieving "carbon neutrality" – that is, to say that future photosynthetic energy will repair that loss. How such a ridiculous hypothesis gained consensus is a mystery – even though it is universally accepted, it has not been proved by any research that I can find – and no-one, who supports it, has been able to find me any. IPCC say that biomass burning can achieve, so called, negative emissions if the gases are captured and stored in some way in a "carbon sump". Farmers and growers can refute the hypothesis, season by season. If we grow a crop, remove it from the farm and make no biomass return to the soil, then soil biomass and energy will shrink, subsequent re-growth will shrink and leaf area presented for photosynthesis will similarly shrink. Year, by year, a tendency to lifelessness will increase and a tendency to life will diminish. The only way we can replace the loss of fertility is by importing it from elsewhere, so that the "elsewhere" is similarly diminished – a hole in the ground with nothing in it. It follows that burning coal with CCS (Carbon capture and storage) is a far, far better thing than burning biomass with CCS. I do not advocate burning coal.

The obsession with carbon as mass in the air, or mass in/on the soil and for a direct cycle between the two, without exchanges of energy, has led to another error. Embedded structures, such as timber buildings are accounted as "carbon sumps" – denying that carbon to the atmosphere! The opposite is true. If we remove life (the tree) from a life-cycle, we shrink both the energy and mass of that cycle. Biomass will be denied to the soil to feed subsequent regrowth and photosynthetic energy of one tree will be removed. The energy of the forest's life-cycle will diminish by the power of that tree and atmospheric CO_2 will increase accordingly. Embedded structures are not a large part of carbon auditing, but future audits may include James Lovelock's carbon sumps, in which large tonnages of biomass are buried – sequestered like coal, oil and gas. It is proposed by many that those sumps will deny carbon to the atmosphere – but they will achieve the opposite – a life-cycle will shrink in mass; in speed of its cycle; in its photosynthetic and regenerative power and lifelessness will increase.

So, here's a thought for economists – that balance of death and life is the measure of a stable economy: one in which economy and ecology become one. Food and soil become one and so human energy (life) and soil become one – also cultural sense of place and soil become one. As lifelessness increases, so the primary economic asset (food-supply) diminishes. It's well to pause here to reflect on our ignorance. A trawling of scientific literature won't help. With regards to biological complexity, we are lost in intellectual chaos. It's plain that the interweaving of an only partly-understood biodiversity is essential for an optimum (that is a durable maximum) bio-energy and mass. Part-understanding is a very dangerous thing. So, in this regard, science is a pleasure, and I'd say, an essential pleasure, but is of little practical use. Application of such ignorance is a definition of stupidity. However, there are other ways towards other kinds of truth - trials and errors of farming and growing bring us close as we can to the truths of dynamic reactions – as I say in the first paragraph – in the deepening, or paling green of foliage – in sustained crop yields. As with much in life, humility and innocence receive the greatest revelations. Of course, the studied scepticism of true science is an attempt at a similar innocence and it can uncover delightful pictures of complexity. But the grower does not need to unravel complexity – structural anthropologists and linguistic philosophers have long-ago failed at that – the grower must only answer the question, what should I do? She can marvel at complexity and enjoy the scientific literature – both of which may increase the diffidence of her footsteps, but her task is to grow the primary economic asset (food) in a way that future growers can attempt the same. All of the above is moral philosophy, it unravels for me, what I should do. Every day, I must do something, by my judgement and cannot wait for scientific corroboration. That, (if you believe in progress) may be centuries away. For myself, I think, we will wait forever, because the answer we seek is the always-illusive complexity – not the addition of its broken-down elements. The broken-down elements are interesting, but of no practical use.

3

Here's another thought – as Richard Douthwaite has taught us, money-flow must shadow energy-flow, so that within the realm of money-exchange it must shadow acceleration due to people. Of course, acceleration due to people also extends beyond the realm of money. We'd regard a lot of what we do to be tainted by money – we would not accept it. So, for many exchanges, money is taboo. In consequence GDP (spending) should be far less than energy due to people. This makes for a more flexible and safe money system, since where money fails, people can step in.

I think, many tragedies that are currently unfolding can be attributed to the enclosure of money as property. As Adam Smith warned, money as property would bring capitalism tumbling around our unprotected ears. I'd go further – all enclosure does the same. Rent for money, status, land, ideas - all idly extract money from the true exchanges of what people do. Rent even extracts money from activities which would otherwise be moneyless. It creates a class system of rent-lords on the one hand and of rent-payers on the other. Rent-lords are plainly what we think of as the middle class, while the rent-payers are in a turmoil of bewilderment, loss of identity, increasing poverty... so that they cannot identify with any class. No wonder we have the dark side of Brexit and of Trump's America – people seeking recognition, belonging and class. Anyway, rent money (debt) has sent money-flow on a trajectory, far beyond acceleration due to people. Not only that, acceleration due to people is sickening in consequence – intelligence of a changing world, ingenuity, dexterity, hope, enthusiasm – all are bled by enclosure – all slowly die, while a tendency for lifelessness accelerates by acceleration due to rent; acceleration due to fossil fuels.

If we suddenly inject an energy far greater than acceleration due to people and a further acceleration of money-flow as a consequence, we can not only have a world where death overwhelms life, but in which lifelessness overwhelms death. Once quietly-sequestered and fossilised life, laid down over many millions of years, has been released by fire to create a plague of human-power. We have wild dis-cultural money and a blanket of atmospheric gases beyond the capacity of merely contemporary life to draw back into her cycles. We can plainly see by the growth of GDPs and GWP that all life will very soon be spent.

Our current GDPs, or GWP are measuring the end, if not of life on Earth, at least of all human cultures and most of the holocenic species of plants, fungi, invertebrates, insects and animals, with which we are familiar.

The largest part of current money-flow, measured by GDP is enabled by the carbon (here I can use the word) once safely-sequestered in the quiet strata of fossilised years. We can also use the rather beautiful word, sequestered for the idle fossils once peacefully reclining in those strata. However, the use of the words, sequestration and carbon, when describing the essentially energetic cycles of life, has led to disturbing errors in climatic models. Perhaps it would always have taken an innocent grower, or a child, to point out those errors. Sadly, and for reasons outlined above with regards to enclosure and here particularly, status enclosure, farmers and growers have been tongue-tied – deferring, quite wrongly to the dignified ignorance of enclosed soil and atmospheric science. The same can be said for the supressed intelligence, which would otherwise be noted by all the trades. Where a tool touches its materials is the closest, in both time and space, that we come to the reactions of those materials. Of course, there are many exceptions to that "dignified ignorance", but on the whole it remains true – certainly in the realms of IPCC, many universities and all government departments. Lazily accepted hypotheses (career-enhancing doctrine) have steered the consensus away from the truth. They've steered cultures away from the soils on which they depend. An easy metaphor – the idle fancies of rent-collecting architects have replaced the functional and elegant buildings which could have risen from the pleasurable and intelligent senses of builders.

Science cannot tell us what to do. Beautiful and detached science has alerted us to a climatic disbalancing, which has been selected by human behaviour. I accept, admire and humbly wonder at the hours of true dedication – the data gathering, the studied patterns emerging... But what we do with new information, brings us to the realms of the effects of causes. It brings us to the trial and error of tools, to ways of life and so to the judgements of moral philosophy – that is, of right and wrong behaviour. One branch of moral philosophy is economics.

Many dedicated scientists have understood this – wearing a sceptical coat for the science, then exchanging it at the end of the day, to wear the moral, pragmatic coat of a whole person. Kevin Anderson and James Hansen are famous examples, but there must be many others. Anyway, I can only admire the science – I sit at her feet – but in the world of economics (of what we do) I can speak on an equal footing with anyone – all trades contribute their insights. Science, being essentially amoral, cannot tell us what to do. Don't forget, although we haven't spent earnest years in gathering and seeking patterns in the data, yet we can all understand the conclusions. We can all delight in the research.

In farming, I defer only to my farm, as she repels, or accepts my behaviour. That is my duty as a commoner. Otherwise, I must defer to others – medical practitioner, plant-breeder, stone-mason, boat-builder, house-builder, forester, turbine maker... There is the trust that should bind a modern society. It is the world of moral commons – of a common history and future. One of the dangers of our current way of life is the legitimisation of "technologists" hiding behind the amoral cloak of science, so that ethics can become detached from actions. Status enclosure consolidates that position, as does career-connected peer-review. Examples include pharmaceuticals, gene technologies, medical practice, pesticides manufacture, "applied climate science", architecture... All these are crafts; arts; tools; technologies... All that we do has an effect and so also a moral. The beauty of science is that she sees from the cultivated position of amorality, which allows for the unexpected to make sense. A "scientist" who leaves that ivory tower, while forgetting to put on her everyday coat of social loves and responsibilities, becomes a dangerous creature, unhampered, libertarian... It is fortunate that true science has an essential humility – a quieted self – so that as she shuts the door of the ivory tower and heads for home, she immediately puts on the moral coat of an ordinary citizen, reclaims her-self and mixes with family and friends.

To function properly, the tool of money cannot be bought and sold. It is a useful tool for more complex energy exchanges – in which unseen actors can contribute. Enclosed money – money as property is irresponsible money. It can create acceleration due to money; to personal power. It can be bought and sold and it can be rented – all without commons of restraint and good behaviour.

Enclosed status (medical practitioner, plant-breeder, solicitor a so on) is irresponsible status. It can charge a rent for that statu which is far beyond a wage for work done. It accumulates money as property and so also achieves acceleration due to money.

Enclosed land is . . . Well, the ill-effects are so well documented that I'll point you to Tom Paine, J S Mill, Henry George . . . to Oliver Goldsmith, *"Ill fares the land, to hastening ills a prey – where wealth accumulates, and men decay."*

This is a chapter about acceleration. We can have acceleration due to people, the effects of skill, ingenuity, dexterity, muscle – people can then rely on acceleration due to gravity – hydro-turbines, pumps, mills and factories, acceleration due to the moon – tidal shipping currents and tidal turbines, acceleration due to biomass – food and building materials, acceleration due to temperature differences – sailing boats, wind turbines pumps and mills, or acceleration due to oxen and horses (I'd hope, within kindly limits).

We can no longer have acceleration due to burning things – either fossil biomass, or living biomass. Perhaps as a first step, we should ask ourselves, how can I live without explosion and fire?

However, we can have acceleration due to fermentation. Since those gases will rise anyway, we can gather them to burn safely, changing one gas for another, minus useful energy.

We can no longer have acceleration due to money; to inequality; to enclosure; to anything, which acts outside the cycles of life, or which breaks our connection to both the time and space of soil, such as fossilised produce of ancient soils. Of course, our cultural history is stuffed full of inequalities, empires, enclosures, deforestation and destructive farming, but now that we have risen so far above the true physics of the world, we must scramble back down by every means we can – or like the baseless fabric of this vision, we'll leave not a wrack behind... Already – we are such stuff as dreams are made on and those in positions of authority almost universally consider that we can make stuff from dreams. The idea of progress is that we make stuff from dreams. Acceleration due to dreams creates just a longer dream.

If we can't have acceleration due to money, then using money – carbon taxes, carbon trading, true-cost accounting, ecosystem services will only endorse what we should rectify. A better way is agreed rationing, re-distribution, and an enthusiastic story-telling of the moral commons of proper behaviour. We don't stop air-travelling, because a tax has made it too expensive, but because it is the wrong thing to do. Once it has been accepted as the wrong thing to do, it can be made illegal. Use of other resources can be similarly rationed, because unfair distribution is plainly wrong – or so the new stories say.

Once upon a time, we could live happily ever after. We can aim for such a time, but first, the plot must pass through a variety of tragedies to get there. In a previous chapter, we chose (from a passing mountebank) future tragedy for a moment of exquisite pleasure. Ain't that a proper tale to tell? It was a dark and stormy night. We said to the tale-teller, tell us a tale. He stepped into the light and began, "It was a dark and stormy night. We said to the tale teller..." You see, we already know what we need to know. We must live through the tragedies we have created. We cannot ask, how can we avoid tragedy? We have already chosen tragedy. Now we must choose the best tragedy and we must live by acceleration due to people; gravity; moon; sun; temperature. But acceleration due to people is primarily dependent on acceleration due to biomass. Our arts, cultural commons and taboos should all (as probably once they were) be focussed on optimum maintenance of that biomass. All the rest are tools to help, or hinder the journey. After all, to become a part of the cycles of life, ours has to be an agriculture, a hunter-gatherer culture, or a mixture of both. At the moment, cultural consensus is choosing minerals, gases, chemical reaction, fire, gravity, the moon, temperature and the linear energy of a lifeless sun.

As an after-thought, most people think that we live in a capitalist society. But how can that be, when capital is rapidly decreasing, and money is rapidly increasing? We live in a casino. We live in a monetarist society. In truth, I can think of no developed economy, which can be called capitalist – which values capital, rather than the spending of it - at least, not since the Thirteenth Century. There's more on capital in later chapters.

****

8

CHAPTER 2 – THE WEALTH OF FIELDS AND NATIONS

As we end bad practice and attempt good practice, so farm and garden soils can accumulate some vital biomass and biodiversity. But that increase in soil biomass will always end at an optimum point, at which the farmer/gardener can only attempt a balance – a stable, living mass. That balance is precarious, because it is subject to human fallibility, unpredictable weather and very human choices, such as attempts to cultivate, or harvest – to salvage something, in unsuitable weathers. Even here, in temperate Wales, such unsuitable weather is becoming more and more frequent. This season we've had extreme rainfall, extreme heat and extreme winds – all of which are likely to grow worse. It's plain that unsuitability will accelerate – that is, current human cultures will be increasingly ill-matched to the weathers, which once sustained them. The lovely yeast of soil, which gave rise to a more or less stable harvest, will be diminished by flood, drought, wind and human desperation. However skilled we are and however hard we struggle, beyond an optimum point, we will not "draw down further carbon" onto our virtuous fields and gardens.

Anyone who raises an eyebrow at the word, desperation, is plainly not a grower, or farmer.

Even in perfect weather, the best husbandry can only aim for balance, while knowing that it will often fall short of that balance – all farming and gardening disrupts the natural ecology it has replaced. I think we should begin with that primary knowledge. We should also assume that we will make mistakes. Our task is to grow food, while causing as little ecological and atmospheric harm as we can. We will cause climate heating and we will disrupt natural systems – knowing that, is the best frame of mind to learn how to limit that disruption.

There are outrageous claims for farming and gardening systems, which "draw down carbon" into their lovely soils. These are often made by the "newly-enlightened", new farmers and growers and by writers and journalists passionately applying a revelatory idea – a permaculture; an agro-ecology - and too easily finding evidence for their own virtue. It is used to promote produce in marketplaces and since it is often a genuine, if deluded aspiration, there are few of the kindly, who'd rock its boat.

If we consider organic as a method which attempts as best it can, to imitate the optimum cycling of organisms, then we have in the word, a fine rule of thumb for all farming and gardening. And it is true that the linear gift of sunlight can repair some very human cracks in our attempted cycles, but only to a point. That point is an optimum (durable maximum) photosynthetic leaf area, much of which will have disappeared down those cracks.

Like sunlight, there are other linear contributions, which are often accepted as a gift from nowhere. They are no such thing. They have come from somewhere - an emptying hole in the ground, a broken organic cycle in some-one else's field, or from a once-vibrant ecosystem, such as a forest.

Many practitioners have made outrageous boasts of soil sequestration by importing large amounts of mulching material. They import from another's impoverished organic cycle. In short, this is either narcissism, or simple anti-social behaviour – it diminishes a common good. If one field receives biomass grown in another field, the sum of the two masses will end as less than the original mass, which had been thriving in the soil and plants of the two separate fields. Although soil biomass will increase in the importing field, it will increase by less than the loss of biomass in the exporting field. The sum of the biomass of both fields will be smaller and Atmospheric CO_2 will increase accordingly. Where is the missing mass? In energy (heat), gas from uncycled fermentation and in leached minerals from the importing field and in cascading diversity and mass of soil fauna and plants in the exporting field.

We could imagine a world without artificial fertilisers, in which the powerful appropriate green wastes and sewage for their high-yielding, money-making fields, while the disempowered struggle to scratch a living. As always with inequity, overall yields will fall, while a few become rich. Overall photosynthesis will fall, along the shrinking soil biomass and increasing atmospheric CO_2.

The human economy is also an organic system. Adam Smith, the moral philosopher, observed, Economies with high wages and low profits achieve the "greatest wealth of nations", while those with low wages and high profits achieve the least.

That equity of wealth distribution, applies equally to both economy and ecology of fields. Of course, a field which is most knit inside the webs of its ecology, achieves greatest economic success. But that success can only be achieved for a community of fields, if so called, wastes (wages) are distributed fairly between all fields. If those biomass/wages are taken by an elite group as profit, then the wealth of the nation of fields will fall.

The greenhouse effect of lifeless gases will increase to the same degree.

Having left fossil mass to lie quietly sequestered in its strata and having ended the burning of living biomass (the lungs of lovely Earth), and having re-arranged our ways of life to do without what those fires and explosions have brought us – suburbia, the family car, aviation... - we must look to Adam Smith's prescription for a bio-massive wealth of nations.

Fields can shrink from the compass of oil-power to the compass of man-power and we must limit growing areas to just our dietary needs – and I'd say, pleasures. Meanwhile, we must let the wilds expand – only the wilds can "draw down carbon". They are Eden. Even so, the wilds will only draw down carbon to an optimum point – but one which will have a greater energy and mass than a neighbouring human culture. Sorrowfully, we cannot escape the Fall. As the poet, Edwin Muir tells us,

> *Time's handiworks, by time are haunted. . . . blossoms of grief and charity bloom from these darkened fields . . . Strange blessings, never in Paradise, fall from these beclouded skies.*

****

11

CHAPTER 3 – A HORTICULTURAL SOCIETY BY WAY OF THE FERNY BRAE

A more horticultural society that learns to garden its land - that retreats into its terrain, while the wilds expand, may still have domestic animals for meat, milk and eggs. We cannot grow annual crops, without fallow, regenerative phases in rotation. My rule of thumb is two years of green manure, or pasture to one year of cropping. Pasturing removes the considerable manual labour of cutting and mulching - I assume a world without both oil and electricity for agricultural machinery. I suspect Earth-limited electricity will stretch only as far as domestic heat, light and some refrigeration. Naturally, we've legs and bicycles for transport and we've direct traction of wind and water for mills, pumps and manufactories. I doubt we can retain the internet.

There is a very old vein of green socialist thinking, which runs deep into medieval times – and almost certainly as deep as the Bronze Age and probably the Neolithic... When Adam delved and Eve span, who was then the gentleman? Here is GK Chesterton describing his hopes for a Distributist movement, which is rooted in that same vein.

> Capitalism is the state run by big business, while communism is big business run by the state. I dream of very many, very small businesses. (from my memory)

That yearning may lie dormant in most of us. And that yearning must flower and fruit if we are to accomplish this massive transformation – re-centring suburbia into towns and villages, so that work and pleasure are walking distance from everyone's door.

Only the intelligent senses of "very many small businesses" could achieve that complexity. We must be parochial, to understand both the specific complexities of terrain and the desires of the parish's people. Good soils, good water and connections of tracks, canals, navigable rivers are all best understood by those who live by them. Those new and old towns and villages, can be ringed with market gardens, corn fields and orchards and the growing must weave its way through the town too, by the specific means of singular ingenious finger-tips. Strange, isn't it? If we come to love our personal terrain – our garden, we more easily love another's.

You say, such a transformation is impossible. Well, yes. It is. But our current ways of life in Europe and America are also impossible. A greening of how we live, or a middle way is just as impossible. So, every road we take is impossible. The future is impossible. So, why not choose the very best – the loveliest impossible route? Why not choose happiness and grit our teeth through what is to come to achieve it?

Actually, a more horticultural society is the most likely road to succeed – the obstacles are political and violent – that is, human obstacles - other people. All other roads are certain to fail, because the obstacles they face are physical - flood, wind, heat and a cascading evaporation of species on which all cultures depend. Try arguing with the tide.

We may think we are doing our bit by paying a little more for an electric car, by recycling, avoiding plastic packaging and by lobbying for a greening of our power supplies – all that, with the social advantage that it is not extreme, or extremist. No-one wants to be "an extremist". However, it's very plain that such a middle way will end in utterly catastrophic heating of our only Earth and utter misery for our own children. It fails right from the start.

However, what if we let an ancient yearning rise in all its romance. It's neither radical, nor extreme as an idea. It's only radical in its effect on the extra-ordinary way we live today. European and American ways of life are so extra-ordinary - so radical that they will draw the final curtain over all human cultures and are set to arrive, by their own boast, at the end history. My vision, (and that of ancestors from every period) is, on the contrary, ordinary, very old and very easily understood. We don't want a radical culture. We want a timeless, conservative one.

To return to our horticultural culture, we've many perennials, such as fruit and nut trees and bushes, but the Land Institute's perennial cereals may offer a less destructive route into a durable terrain. But still, they mean harvesting the whole plant, both grain and straw (as with annual cereals) and so may similarly need a regenerative phase – perhaps a season or two of grazing?

Fallow, regenerative phases mean that animals can add to the complexity of a cycle, but are also limited by its plant biomass. We can add pleasurably, to the whole, while having no malignant ecological effect. The same desire for bread and beer also creates the special, but rationed pleasures of milk, butter, cheese, eggs and meat. I think it unlikely that we can maintain additional pastures purely for meat and milk.

Anyway, very many, small prairie fields could remain within our horticultural mind-set. The scythe is a pleasant tool and scything cereals is not hard work – unlike mixed meadow grasses. Grains are also precious, because they can be stored from good years into bad and they are very light – only 15% water, so that they can be easily transported between surplus and scarcity of regions. Thus, they are useful in both time and space. Anyway, as of old, communities can come together for the harvest. Many hands.

Here in temperate UK, many of those rolling acres of grassland, were first enclosed to remove people from the land and replace them with sheep. Sheep made wool-money for the few –they bled dry the true economy of people hefted to their land and became a blueprint for all monopolies and most dispossessions. Those grasslands can be returned to their natural state as woodland – woodland for photosynthesis, the return of the wilds and for timber. We'll need timber and we'll not need that 80% of Welsh lamb for export. Of course, we'll have no land to spare to feed biomass boilers, broiler houses, batteries and feed lots. What of hill and upland farming communities? Some traditions go back to at least the Bronze Age and some older still – They can adopt the same horticultural mind-set for better soils and of course, forestry and its trades, will provide more employment than sheep ever could. If wool is re-valued as it should be, then sheep may play a part in a new complexity, but it is not only hill communities, whose lives must turn upside down – it is all of us.

Just as all of us must dramatically reduce our consumption of things in general, so we must dramatically reduce our consumption of land. Those extensive pastures, which many now claim, "draw down

carbon" and turn inedible-to-people grasses into valu
are profligate pastures creating consumerist luxuries. I
and let as much land as we can, return to the sound
sights of the wild. We'll still have those luxuries, b
limits of the rotations of a horticultural mindset and they will be
special – set aside for feast days and holidays.

Now, let's consider this - Old Socialism, Old Tory, Old Liberal (Wig)
and so on, would have been similarly connected to soil, materials,
labour, the trades – diverse ways of both urban and rural living.
They'd find a common truth in material things. Their dispute would
be a similarly ancient one – in distribution of materials and between
classes and power structures; between urban and rural. They'd
share the same evidence of their own eyes – climate and ecological
catastrophe, empty holes in the ground, which once held resources,
increasingly lifeless soils, wealth and poverty both accelerating
wildly, and no-one in control of the ship of fools.

They might well share a common acceptance of fair rationing (war-
footing) and of an urgent need for utterly changed behaviour. At any
rate, they'd share the same horror as the great ship, the Newly
Marketed Centre Corporate Green Ground, embarked without
touching the ground, or without noting winds, currents, tides, or ice
bergs (unfortunate metaphor).

It is easy to be enlightened to the virtues of the centre and very easy
to ridicule the en-darkened edges – that is, the old dark ways of
rivers, trees, fields, bird songs, crops, workshops, pianos, wild
flowers, mountains, frying onions, pub songs, parishes, gravity,
tides, passing seasons, harbours and people.

Nigel Farage's pint glass has been a potent image. It is attractive,
human-sized and is not measured in statutory litres. People are not
wrong to yearn for a good life in a simple world. That Nigel Farage
and Boris Johnson both represent something quite different – and
horribly different, while presenting such homely images, does not
negate that genuine yearning. Farage/Johnson represent total
deregulation of the same corporate levitation, which is supported by
New Labour, Liberal Democrat and Greens. All support the
corporate levitation, but the "centrists" would negotiate consumer
and environmental protections within it. Neither extreme right of
Johnson/Farage, nor the status quo of the prosperous middle-

ground will protect themselves from that same corporate self-destruction.

G K Chesterton stood, pint in hand like Falstaff in merry England, or Robert Burns with a jug of wine, lying in the heather, or William Barnes, *"I've got two fields and I don't care what squire mid have a better share."* Or let's follow Thomas the rhymer under the hill –

> *See ye not yon braid, braid road that winds among the lily leven? – That is the path to wickedness, that some ca' the road to heaven. – And see ye not yon narrow road, s' thick beset with thorn and briar? – That is the path to righteousness, though after it few enquire. – But see ye not yon bonny road that winds among the ferny brae? That is the path to fair Elfland, where thou and I this night maun gae.*

When all roads fail, choose the bonny road. It is right because our souls will choose it and because yet half visible truth has long ago chosen it.

I like to think that the old Socialist, Conservative and Green movements are all closer to a true median ground which stands on (and in) soil, biodiversity and physics, than the currently and powerfully marketed idea of a centre. They are closer in their diverse ways, to the model for all economies. They are closer to the household – to everyday personal behaviour. Meanwhile, the powers behind government, corporation and bank entice left, right and green to their marketed middle ground and to an illusion of franchises in the world of power. The same powers wear enticing left, right and green clothing which is then adopted my many in those groups (such as UK Green Parties), who propose that they are moving towards a reconciliatory centre. They are not. They are endorsing utterly amoral and destructive power. They are abandoning "family values" and embracing a kind of amorality for all, into which any morality can fit and then argue its corner. That world of power is also an idea. It has no substance. The substance, once again is in the billions of small purchases and in the millions of accepted wages... Anyway, we now have an almost overwhelming fantasy world of New Green, New Labour, New Liberal and New Tory all of whom lobby for the "reality" of a corporate supplied consumerism and against the "delusion" of egalitarian and convivial settlements in real and utterly finite landscapes.

Let's stop spending the idea into reality and then look to each other (Really, we all know it's true) – and one, by one, take the bonny road.

****

CHAPTER 4 – A SOCIETY IN WHICH WORK AND PLEASURE ARE WALKING DISTANCE FROM EVERYONE'S DOOR

We need a society in which both work and pleasure are walking distance from everyone's door. That is the foundation of our task to allow the revival of other species and to allow the lungs of Earth to re-find their balance. I cannot see another remedy. Most people profoundly disagree. Wild polemics advise that we can green our current ways of life, while friends of mine say that their chosen way of farming will "draw down carbon", others say, Yes, – very nice, but dream on. while still others say, look how far we've advanced, technology will continue to advance and find a way.

This is what I say.

We need to re-centre suburbia, revive derelict town and village centres and shut-down corporate-supplied consumerism. Rather than green our loud energy demands, we must hush the noise and begin to watch and listen. We must shrink our needs to fit within what we learn from that natural lesson. Our most destructive activity is transport. Greening that destruction is futile. We must remove the need for it as much as we can.

And we can replace the high-powered internet and its connected global transport with good conversation, concerts, theatres, pub gossip and sing songs, musical instruments, books, market squares, proper shops, workshops and cafes spilling onto the street. We can replace unreality with reality. That reality includes safe and convivial car-free roads, where people can stroll at leisure and children can play as children should. And we can bring market gardens into town and revive private gardening and allotments. As we remove the old infrastructures, so we also remove dependency. Dependency is a soul-sapping weight. Liberated, we can set pleasures, ingenuity and dexterity free. These arguments are old as the hills.

Which is why this needs little explanation. The transformation is from an extraordinary fossil-powered levitation and back to very ordinary and easily-understood solid ground. It's also fortunate that the ordinary contains all that is marvellous – seasons, sights, scents, sounds. We need no advice from academics, consultants, architects, journalists, or government officials to achieve it. In truth, that hierarchy of professional (and deluded) monopolies has played the major part of our crazy levitation. What's more, from that elevation it has reached down and extracted crippling rents from those who still generate real economic activity. If I need a solicitor, or doctor, or if I need planning permission for my self-built house, I must bring my £6 per hour to pay for their £300 per hour. I pay for a class system. I pay for idle education by my physical labour. That degree of educated idleness can only exist by the cash-generating power of fossil fuels. Of course, it also existed and existed perniciously, but with a smaller power, before the arrival of fossil fuels.

Sometimes, reality will produce scarcity and surplus – such necessary trade can be managed (if we work at it) by canal, navigable river and the sea. Sail trade is tried and tested. Even though you say, "Dream on mate", it is the only trade which fits physical reality. It can also revive coastal communities. Can we maintain the railway? Only trial and error will tell. Certainly, it must be efficient rail – that is, slow rail. How far will durable electricity stretch? Nobody knows. Its first uses must be domestic. That may well prove its limit, but perhaps it will stretch a little further. Certainly, I don't know. In any case, uncertainty is the best frame of mind to receive enlightening fragments of certainty.

Fossil fuels have lifted humanity high above the Earth on a wild ride to self-destruction. What's more, they have not brought happiness. Our species had evolved to find its place amongst all the other species. Firstly, agriculture came too fast for our deeper selves to keep pace – the inherited moral structures that form family, community and their settlement inside the natural world, were often overlain by that new reality. Thus, moral structures became both strained and exploited. In many instances, we could justly call that new agricultural reality - unreality. Throughout history, (and no doubt, pre-history) many agricultural communities had pillaged their soils and so themselves, even before the magnificent power of fossil fuels levitated our half-unreal agriculture into utter, unmitigated unreality. By agriculture, I mean a culture of roads, villages, towns and cities – of specialised trades – all of which are enabled by the specialist cultivation of fields. Today, in spite of the marvels of aviation; of the internet and so on, we remain an agriculture.

A society in which both work and pleasure are walking distance from everyone's door can remain an agriculture – or as I shall pursue, a more horticultural society, into which animals can beneficially contribute. I think our settlements must retract as the wilds expand.

I carry Utopia with me like an imaginary harbour light, or the evening star. Our cultural voyage cannot embark without hope. Yet, looking at the evidence, there is now no future for humankind – the heating is more rapid than all peer-reviewed predictions. Looking at my family, friends and neighbours, it is plain that we will not achieve the fast (immediate) mutation of social behaviour necessary to live within planetary means. Yet hope is something different. It is anchored, transcending time, to its final leading light. Says Thomas Traherne –

> You never enjoy the world aright, until the sea itself floweth in your veins - until you are clothed with the heavens and crowned with the stars." And know yourself to sole heir to all the universe – and more so, since all others are sole heirs also.

Yes, our journey will devise many compromises in the face of both human and natural obstacles. But the thing is, as we set off again, having necessarily compromised, our renewed guiding light must remain Utopia. Compromising a pragmatic compromise always leads to hopeless disaster. After all, Utopia is Nowhere. It always leads to hope.

****

CHAPTER 5 – SPENDING AND SELLING IDEAS INTO REALITY

Yes. Let's stop spending, or enacting polemical ideas into reality. A corporation exists on two plains – one is a polemical idea – an advertisement - the other is the many small purchases, which create its reality. A corporation is a sold fantasy, which becomes actual by my spending. Has anyone ever seen a corporation? Yes, you may say, they are very real – you receive real wages for real work done. You are a real cog in its wheel and your work-place is a highly visible concrete and glass structure. I say, that you too have been spent into existence and what's more, you could just as easily be unspent and in search of a new identity – hopefully inside the true physics of soil, forests, fields, rivers, seas, workshops and people.

Currently successful political parties are those which lobby for and disperse that same corporate advertisement. Votes follow the money and money follows the votes – those many small purchases, which make a reality. Softly and silently (I apologise to the poet) commercial corporations are sliding into government. Most politicians angle their profiles, so that they, in the same way, will be personally spent and balloted into power.

Politics and consumerism have become so entwined that the ballot has become little more than another consumer-choice – a consumer choice within the same corporate supply.

Here in the UK there is only one large political group, which stands on more or less physical ground – that surrounding Jeremy Corbyn. Just about every newspaper, radio/television station and political party is utterly focused on destroying it. If they don't destroy it, they may be un-spent from existence by the contrary power of reality. You ask, "What of the Green Party?" I say, it has very recently levitated into what it sees as the advantageous world of corporate European power. Rest in Peace.

How can something, which has no existence, become physical by the power of money? Well, many things do, such as class structures in which real money is extracted from the real economy of the real household to finance my absolutely abstract class status as dentist, GP, solicitor, architect... That extraction could be called rent and it could be called extortion. All enclosures do the same. They extract rent for money, land, status, or ideas and weaken real economic activity - that is the real goings on of people and the land.

Actually, instead of spending an abstract corporate polemic into reality, why not find a reality and describe, extol the value of its existence. Why not extol existence into existence? Then, why not un-spend a corporation into abstraction again? It is easy to spot politicians who have been bought into existence. They speak like robots – or puppets on a mysterious string. Often, coming from nowhere, they suddenly appear on every front page, fulfilling, of course someone else's purpose. Here in the UK, one of those chosen in that way, is the media-groomed, very young Liberal Democratic Party leader, Jo Swinson. I suspect the puppeteer is the media baron Rupert Murdoch. Once she has fulfilled her purpose (exacerbation of the labour Party division over Europe) the strings will be cut and the puppet will disappear.

But it is not only the corporate fantasy that is sold into reality. On "our" side of the argument much that is doctrine, is repeated so much that it can mutate into a consenting hypothesis. That such hypotheses are untested is forgotten in the passionate noise of the original doctrinal polemic. In the battlefield we grow to encourage and protect our comrades in arms.

Then, an untested hypothesis can be used to create further chapters to the doctrine – with reference "to the science" – quietly forgetting that the science has never existed.

Gunnar Rundgren has an excellent article
https://www.resilience.org/stories/2019-08-21/small-farms-dont-produce-most-the-of-the-worlds-food-but-they-could-produce-all/ ,
which unpicks the polemic that "Small farms produce 70% of the world's food". They don't. It doesn't help either our argument, or our task that they *should* produce all the world's food, by manipulating figures to show that they already produce 70%. The claim originates from a report by the ETC Groups in 2009, 'Who Will

Feed Us?' Now, most of the small farmers and growers I speak to, have that figure indelibly imprinted as a motivational slogan.

I've come across that same brick wall - that line of shouldered arms and have been labelled both schismatic and also of having "no peer review". Pointing out that the doctrine in question similarly has no peer review and has never been tested, will have no effect, because the doctrine has become sacred and I have become schismatic.

This particular doctrine is the foundation for sequestration calculations of the IPCC, Zero Carbon Britain 2030 and almost all academic publications besides. No one can show me where and how it has been tested and I'm fairly sure that it never has been tested. I think that the hypothesis, now mutated from an original doctrine, whose source seems untraceable, is possibly (I think extremely likely to be) the cause of the vastly underestimated rate of climate change.

Here it is as given to me by one of the authors of Zero Carbon Britain 2030 in response to my inquiry –

> *If biomass is burned, the chemistry is more or less reversed, and the original energy and raw material (CO_2 and water) are released. There is then no net gain or loss of CO_2, which is why biological fuels are considered to be carbon neutral.*

That is to say, we can burn a crop, turning its living, energetic mass into dead gas, small ashes and powerful energy and then wonderfully as virgin birth, green shoots will rise from somehow immortal, yet still living soil to spread their leaves and photosynthesise as before. Soil is proposed to be as the cauldron of Ceridwen – though we regularly devour the contents, it will never be empty. That the doctrine is unbelievable probably gives potency to the belief.

The tragedy is that the hypothesis is tested season by season by millions - even billions of farmers, growers and gardeners and by scores of agricultural research bodies, which publish crop yield figures. Yet, specialist monopolies are so sure of the sanctity of their enclosures that such simple truth is forbidden entry. After all, careers would be on the line and the credibility of researchers and university departments seeking funding would be shredded by winds of ordinary common sense. Well, Amen, I say. Professional status enclosure, not only wrecks economies by rent, but it also monopolises truth and so spreads unchallenged delusion. Peer review has mutated to career review, in the same way that doctrine can mutate to hypothesis.

Here's some simple truth – a truth at the finger-tips of every farmer and gardener –

In addition to the gas released from burning a crop for energy (about the same as from burning coal), we also create the following negative effects.

1. If we grow a crop, burn it, and so make no biomass return to the soil, then the following seasons crop will be smaller, because the biomass of soil fauna will be similarly smaller.

2. Reduced crop yield means reduced photosynthesis, so that the linear contribution of sunlight to the otherwise cyclic nature of life in our garden will be similarly reduced. Atmospheric CO_2 will increase in consequence.

3. We could import minerals (fertilisers) from a consequently emptying hole on the ground and so maintain crop yield, but still, soil biomass would decrease. Furthermore, it would decrease more rapidly than in point 1, because artificially-increased plant biomass would "mine" the natural mineralisation of soil fermentation and so further diminish soil fauna/biomass (sequestration). (I leave aside the negative effects on the biomass and diversity of soil fauna, of pesticides, fungicides, herbicides, growth regulators, genetic manipulation and of malignant effects of fertilisers themselves)

4. If we take biomass from our garden and bury it deep - sequestered from the cycles of life – that is, sequestered like coal, oil and gas – then, similarly to point 1, we will diminish soil life, stunt regrowth and shrink photosynthesis. Consequently, we will increase atmospheric CO_2. Gas, which would have been drawn down by an optimum photosynthesis, will remain in the atmosphere. The same applies to "embedded structures", such as timber buildings.

5. Removing biomass without a return of biomass, slows both the speed and energy of a cycle, while also of course, shrinking its biomass. Speed and energy are often missing from carbon-cycle models. We can observe changing speed by the deepening, or paling green of foliage. Imagine watching the flow of biomass in the same way that we watch the flow of water in a river. The volume in front of us remains the same, until we consider time – litres per second – and energy – driven at 32ft per second sq. We must also consider the speed of flow and energy in biomass. Life is energetic and so is the contribution of sunlight.

The linear contribution of sunlight is dependent on the gathering power and mass of life cycles.

To continue my (imperfect) analogy, if we remove a mass of water from the river, the water will slow, as the smaller mass spreads more quietly between its unchanged banks. If we remove biomass from a field, life will slow as it spreads more quietly across its unchanged acreage. Regrowth will slow. Photosynthesis will slow. More time will be needed to achieve the same yield from both sunlight and plant mass. Days and seasons have absolute limits. Time, as the philosophers say, waits for no biomass.

Actually, crop-yield teaches all we need to know about manipulated organic cycles. To test the IPCC hypothesis, we can go to the great mass of research into crop yields. Otherwise we can record the goings on of our gardens. A simple record is enough.

IPCC and almost all others propose that carbon sumps and embedded structures remove CO.2 from the atmosphere. That delusion is a part of almost all climate models. They also propose that burnt biomass from an unchanged cropping system ("non land-use change") is Carbon neutral. Moreover, it is proposed that if emitted carbon is captured and stored, (CCS) we can achieve the miracle of negative emissions. That delusion is also part of almost all climate models.

Burnt biomass with CCS at proposed rates will very soon strip most forests from the Earth, while turning fertile soils towards desert.

Burnt coal with CCS would leave those forests and soils to live and breathe.

Coal and biomass burning emit more or less the same quantity of greenhouse gases, but biomass burning also shrinks both carbon sequestration and the regeneration of biomass. It follows that burning coal is very much safer than burning biomass. If we consider a transition to "zero carbon" (it must be rapid), then first, we must stop burning biofuels, then coal, then oil, then gas. *

I don't recommend burning coal.

Biofuel crops for transport fuels - oil seeds, sugar cane and so on, have the same ill effect.

I do not apologise for repeating the above, which I've put regularly in print, in various forms since 2005.

* *Anaerobic fermentation from "wastes" provides useful gas – especially for domestic use, while also returning biomass "digestate" to the soil. Fermentation happens anyway and everywhere and whatever we do. With AD we gather methane (mostly), burn it and release CO_2. But, I don't think we have the acreage for AD crops to displace food crops, since we must do all we can to reduce that area, and so let the wilds expand.*

****

CHAPTER 6 – EXODUS

Consider this: everything we do to support current ways of living is so destructive that it will cause the end for human cultures as we know them. The jobs we do; taxes we pay; purchases we make, all contribute to self-destruction.

To lobby for improvements; efficiencies; for a greening of that way of life, gives it further credence and worse – a greater longevity. By that lobbying, we endorse destruction and we signal support for a more efficient but still destructive status quo.

The answer is a mass exodus towards another way of life. For me, it is a journey from the extra-ordinary to the ordinary – from anxiety to sweet relief – from the end of history to history again – and from a crazy, fossil-fuelled levitation, to a specific ration of time inside a measured allotment of space – palpable things, which weigh easily on my understanding and which I can love, share, smell, taste, touch, hear and see.

It is an exodus from cyber money to real money; from an internet of illusions to the physics of things; from travelling without travail to the obstacles and rewards of terrain – rivers, hills, seas, peoples. Our journey will pass from dependent consumerism to personal management of a fair share of time and space. We inherit that share in the passages of time and we are tasked to bequeath its undiminished space as our time also passes. We fulfil an ephemeral role, which was similarly held by generations of ancestors. We occupy but one small human space in the larger and grander flow of history, but the grand is made up of all its individuals. Past action created my ration, just as my present action creates (or diminishes) future rations.

The idea of an allotment, or a ration is very different from ideas of limits, or borders.

A ration is both physical and spiritual – my allotted garden is full of wonders, changing seasons, visiting species, evidence of personal histories on a terrace here; a tree there; many stories and moral lessons attached to the physics of things. I see the actions of ancestors embedded there too, as clearly as I can read ancient words emerging from a page. Similarly, both my allotted house and my allotted workplace are repositories for memory; obligation; celebration and are catalysts for new ingenuities to fit the inevitability of changing times. My allotted time and space are fluid, ever-changing and also changeable by my actions.

The ancient term we have for such allotments is the common.

On the other hand, limits and borders, remain as thin lines, which we cannot cross. They can't be loved – only defended. They sometimes appear inside the common as taboo – that is, things which we cannot say, or do, but more generally they destroy the common. We have liberty inside a border to do as we choose – home as castle – profession as castle – money as castle, and where we override another's morality, we can become lawfully immoral. Monopolies of land, profession and money, exclude the specific ingenuity, dexterity and sensual intelligence of others. The consumer is limited only by the thin line at the edge of her borrowing and spending power. Her right as money-property holder overrides moral commons of proper behaviour.

The terms we have for borders and limits are enclosure and property. Inside my property, I am libertarian – I can be profligate, selfish, cruel, or (I defer), kind as I choose. Enclosures are untouched by nature – they have no nature. But they can be bought and sold, or violently lost and won.

****

The now accustomed measure of economic success is GDP, which in recent times has been mostly composed of spent assets. Tragedies of war and natural disaster, as well as foolish and profligate behaviour, plus usury and rent, all lead to a swelling of GDP. If we applaud GDP as a measure, then we applaud those things. If we applaud a shrinking of GDP, we may seem to applaud the shrinking of those things, but nevertheless we still signal approval of the measure itself (de-growth of GDP). For instance, GDP measures the expenses of climate heating as positive.

We may reason that to fit within the means of a terrain, we must shrink that spending – we must achieve rapid de-growth to just the point that our limited means will provide. And yet, we can see that degrowth will cause "economic", or rather, casino collapse. Casino collapse (of banking, share and stock markets and currencies) will also cause real economic collapse – this is, of manufacturing, labour, social infrastructures...

So, our exodus must be from GDP to a different measure – from the spending of assets to the maintenance of assets. Our hope is not for the casino to degrow to a point – an apparently positive end within the same measure – but for the casino to collapse, while at the same time, we have built a new life boat economy defined by new measures to rescue the falling fragments of the old. I say life boat, because there is unavoidable chaos ahead. The life boats can then deposit us on durable ground.

Pursuit of the degrowth of an impossible way of life, does not change the way of life, it merely presents it with new limits. In any case, enforced degrowth is impossible without chaos and human misery.

If, like any business, or household, we measure community success by measuring assets (not the spending of them), then we enter a brave new world of possibility. The Inland Revenue measures my annual household income as assets in year two, minus assets in year one. In the same way, so can a national accountant. But then, if we ask the questions, what are assets? and, what do we mean by assets? – we surely leave the amoral world of property and enclosure to enter the both pragmatic and spiritual world of the always moral commons. The study of economics is, after all, a branch of moral philosophy.

Everything I do has an effect and so also a moral. My property enclosure allows me to deny that truth. GDP as a measure also denies that truth. It liberates bad behaviour.

What are my assets? I say, family, friends, good air and water, birdsong, green leaves, scent of flowers, ancestral music and literature, good cooking, musical instruments, pubs, libraries... Some have monetary value, some not. All have moral value.

Do those assets survive from year one to year two? Even though they may not and become lost in war, famine, or flood, GDP may still soar, and by the same expenses of war and post disaster re-building that those lost assets bring. It does not measure destroyed assets as a negative. It does not register the weeping.

GDP does not measure even monetarily-valued assets – furniture, tools, property, or existing social infrastructures, such as electricity cables, water and sewage systems, hospital buildings, roads, harbours, bridges, work-shops, houses– it knows neither the presence, nor the lack of them. They become visible only when they are sold. Monetarist UK governments, such as Margaret Thatcher's, Tony Blair's and all others since, have paraded rosy "balance sheets" by exchanging such assets for money (privatisation). However cheaply they are sold they will add to such "balances" and also add to GDP. Asset stripping is a well-tried method to stave off bankruptcy – or to make hidden subsidiary companies (otherwise known as favours to a friend) rich by the cheapness of the purchase. But a bad end is inevitable! Yes, if GDP is presented as a measure of the good, then a bad end is inevitable.

The government of Bhutan has introduced us to an "Economics of happiness". From Latin America, we have learnt "Buen Vivir". "Liberation Theology" teaches much the same, while the thoughts of Ivan Illich require urgent revival. Then we have the lean economics of David Fleming.

They all point to our first steps of exodus – the pragmatic answers to the question, what is happiness?

****

Those who argue for de-growth of our current way of life, perhaps combined with a green new deal for more durable infrastructures, must be careful what they wish for. If it supports the same, but less profligate and more green way of life inside the same old world of amoral enclosures, then it is doomed to failure – more money to fund the impossible - flood, famine, storm...

However, if a green new deal is diverted to support the pack-horses of Exodus, with provisions for the journey and for the final settlements, then money can mutate to an asset again. Money, which has once spent, or extracted real assets can be returned to the common from where it gained its destructive power by bleeding that common. Like Tom Paine's land value tax, which returned enclosure-generated money to the common, a green new deal can be seen as restorative justice.

****

Here is a very simple truth – only good personal behaviour can bring humanity as a whole (literally) down to Earth, and to living within a ration of Earth. All intelligence of the goings on of life, must first pass through unique and singular senses. There is no corporate, or consensual way listening, scenting, seeing... What's more that intelligence is specific to its time and space. Cultural adaption is specific to its terrain and to its time in history, and so is personal in the same way. Of course, personal action will be in, or towards concert with others. We are a social species. We love to share intelligence and we love to live and work together. We are empathetic and sympathetic – personal good (or, I suppose bad) behaviour is contagious.

Political behaviour can be useful if it speaks in defence of an established, or establishing way of life. It is up to us to establish that life, only then, can we defend it – that is, we must have something, or at least the infancy of something, to romance others to join it.

Otherwise, we punt just another idea in the greater casino of ideas. We say, that others must distort their realities to an alien idea. Of course, hierarchies, armies, police, secret police, manipulated ballots, commercial advertisements and persuasive newspaper barons, do that as a matter of course. It has not been productive. Its purpose is destructive.

Our purpose is to escape that course towards the truths of a human settlement within its ration of larger nature.

However, there is much that can hinder that personal journey, which we may need to repel by argument, ballot, or violence, but unless we are personally on the road and unless we know what it is that we defend, then political, or violent, or so-called, non-violent action will be futile.

So, if we are on, or are about to step on the road, or even simply dreaming of the road, then political action may assist the journey. Certainly, unless the so-called body-politic can see our journey as a

31

palpable thing, then we flaunt a mere idea, which can be neither emulated, nor shared - nor truly attacked.

****

So, our extinction rebellions must be primarily against ourselves. Without our billions of small purchases, the corporation would not exist. We must urgently create an economy amongst ourselves, which can survive the crash of banking, stock and share markets, currencies and everything which depends on them. To be sure, the richer we are, the more planetary harm we command, but from where do those riches come, but from ourselves? Our argument is with people – with the vicious rent extraction practised by doctors, lawyers, architects and so on – many of whom may well take part in the extinction rebellion. It is no accident that those status enclosures usually define themselves as a practice – medical practice, law practice, architectural practice and so on. We argue for an exodus from the economic drainage of such practices. When Adam delved and Eve span.... Once upon a time, professionals professed. Now, as a casino has replaced an economy, professional means one who has enclosed a trade and can charge rent for it. It means one who must never profess, but must be reserved, taciturn discrete... To profess is now labelled, unprofessional.

Arise ye professionals and profess – because you are currently the very foundation of our suicidal, but peer-reviewed, rentier casino.

I am an atheist, raised by two atheist parents, but surely our exodus must be a religious exodus? Don't we join the swelling caravans to protect the sacred – good soils, clear water, vibrant forests, teeming seas...? Are not invisible ancestors spurring us forward in shame and ain't that an invisible future I hear calling through palpable veils of richly-spun illusion? Certainly, for myself, I feel my mother and father looking down and it is hard to bear the steady eyes of children. How can ephemeral powers compare to that? And how can ephemeral power compare to this thought – my present action creates the future?

Are not clear springs and ancient woods invisible to GDP? What calls us forward has no peer review and the language of that calling is the language of the Koran; of the Bible... We respond at the deeper level of fine music, poetry, prose and painting and of the primary lessons of childhood for what is deeply right and deeply

32

wrong. That lesson is currently invisible to journalists and politicians, but as the saying goes, they are people too – especially in the small hours of the night.

When I say fine music and so on, a simple folk song, or a two-up, two-down house can be fine things. Ancestry calls for present action to create a future. It says culture is what I do. It is the voice of the commons. Our exodus is from the ennui of enclosure, to the ingenuity, dexterity and conviviality of the common.

****

CHAPTER 7 – REBELLION

Let's resume – our course is towards a society in which both work and pleasure are walking distance from everyone's door. Such a society, is stitched into folk memory. It is very easily understood. Only a hundred years ago, it was the normal for nearly everybody and it is still normal for billions of people outside Europe and North America.

Much that is hateful in contemporary life is a direct result of road transport and the family car – scarring settled communities and driving people to the desolation of retail park and suburban ennui. Concreted ribbons of murderous (they do have intent) speed, force childhood games away from the natural world and into rootless electronic phantasy – adults too. To electrify such a world, will not change its evil and anyway a renewing Earth does not have anywhere near the capacity to produce such power.

Any proposal for behaviours necessary to shrink the human greenhouse effect, must begin with the assumption that the bicycle and the sailing boat provide the limits to "technological advancement" in transport. If they don't have that assumption, then they live in the twentieth century delusion that energy is infinite.

Proposals for a transition back to that ancient and ordinary way of life must first pass through what we've got, to travel to where we must. Many are attempting the journey, but most of us are failing. We fail because we must embark not only individually, but also as a community.

Meanwhile the very first step is to abandon aviation immediately and absolutely. That is easy, and comes with little social complication. Those who haven't, are clearly not serious. Sadly, very many "environmental" campaigners, film-makers, writers and gurus, fly so often that they must be among the most destructive people on Earth. Let's begin by forgetting them. They deserve no credence. They must have no understanding of greenhouse causes, or how could they bear to do it? Otherwise, they have differing reasons, such as narcissism, career prospects, diminished social conscience, or diminished sense of truth.

You see, we have quickly and simply disposed of the bulk of the academic and political literature. Let's not waste further time trawling through it.

For myself as a farmer, and by means of street markets and farmers' markets, I have attempted to connect with places where work and pleasure are walking distance from everyone's door. But as town centres become increasingly desolate, so farmers' markets also decline. Towns and their trades have declined, as oil-powered retail parks and super markets have expanded.

Meanwhile, many of those who would otherwise seek my produce, are lured away from both their local town and from my market stall, by the ease of "ethical" internet shopping. Not only the now familiar super market delivery van, but also smaller couriers carrying organic box scheme orders, suck dry those older and more durable communities of trade and the trades; of pubs, shops, cafes, concert halls, theatres and libraries, which for centuries, and without oil, or coal have made up what we called, town. Of course, coal and timber have fed the domestic fireplace for some of those centuries. But that's our central problem – the production of domestic heat. We'll have no electrical energy to spare for transport.

We have become deluded by both oil and the internet. There is no future for either of them. I use the internet to "post" this piece of writing. I hope, it is a posting in transition. If we live within Earthly means, then we cannot maintain the vast electrical energy needed for the internet. What's more, wonderful as it is, it has not brought happiness. I speculate it has brought the opposite.

But consider this - since internet shopping draws people away from centres for durable shopping, it cannot be a step of transition, rather it is a place awaiting evacuation. The same can be said of super markets stocking organic, or fair-trade goods – those goods are not a step of transition – rather thy await evacuation to something which is more truly on the road. The "virtue" of organic produce cannot be used, in the monk-pardoner manner, as dispensation for the vice of the super market – in which so much vice, mixed with an equal weight of virtue becomes indulged – leaving no stain on the character. Such moral accountancy leaves us heading to mass extinction of very many familiar species and to three degrees of warming fast. It leaves power in the hands of irresponsive, amoral and often immoral monopoly. Consumer choice for a greening of the super market will not change that trajectory.

Similarly, an electric car does not change the trajectory. The good of electric does not balance the bad of the car. In any case we have insufficient non-destructive means to produce the electricity needed for either the car's propulsion, or its manufacture. Domestic heat, light, refrigeration and cookery will use most of the electricity we can produce – and then we can hope for some leeway to produce ceramics, metal-working and so on. It is foolish to seek ways to green existing transport, when the simple solution is to remove the need for most of it.

It is a deep sadness that my own road to transition is crumbling around me. I have loyal customers, who I've known for twenty years and more and I am loyal to them. Like me, they grow older and dwindle by the ageing process. Younger people do not replace them. It is a false assumption that street markets are full of hipster dudes. They are not (at least not here in Wales). The great bulk of my sales are to retired people, who also like to cook – practical people who once held a trade, who garden – who hate pesticides - who are self-reliant – who have sheds full of tools – who fix things when they are broken – and are as far from hipsterism as can be imagined. They are from both the left and right of politics, but are connected by something deeper. I like them – to me, though most do not profess to be "green", they are the vanguard of a true "climate movement".

Our small farm (89 acres) produces vegetables of every kind, soft fruit, apples, apple juice, beef and lamb – all of which are sold on our market stalls. We also grow some cereals. Increasingly, we return from market with unsold produce. That cannot continue. We are hollowed out at the same rate that town centres are hollowed out and as, I speculate, a true climate movement is being hollowed out.

If I said, opportunistically - town centres are dead, we must follow the new crowd to the internet – by courier, drive-to distribution "hub" and electronic money, I would also be saying – fuck transition to vivacious and convivial centres, I'll go where the new crowd go. I think that new crowd are heading for oblivion, albeit, peer-reviewed oblivion.

Many of my organic, agro-ecological, perma-cultural friends are following the money. Once, a friend set up a box scheme on rented, well-chosen and good land, using amateur gardening skills. Within three or four years, having had large "rural development" grants for machinery and promotion, she became both stressed and bored and sold the business and machinery for mere money – the community's tax money. Instead she took an English literature course. My son met her husband a year or so later, and he asked, are you still doing that? We've moved on ages ago... Yes, I'm afraid we are still rooted in our fields – as Thomas Hardy noted, *though dynasties pass*. I must add that I love the true amateur – that is, one who loves. I hope we are amatory on the farm. Certainly, it cannot be abandoned without breaking the heart.

I support the school strike for climate – it is a marvellous thing. Moral children ask immoral adults to act morally. About extinction rebellion – I have sympathy, but also have doubts. Adults demand that other adults behave properly. But are those who demand it of others, also demanding it of themselves? Are they truly adult? Extinction Rebellion could be much like consumerism in which dependants demand changes to the provisions they receive from government and corporation, but are determined to remain in that dependent childhood. If they remain in dependent childhood, then god help the real children.

If those in the rebellion are also attempting to change the ways that they live and work – if they are also rebelling against themselves – then a demand that government and corporation remove obstacles from that path is productive and genuine. Many in the movement are doing just that, but a very high proportion are not. Others are demanding a greening of their work and play places – which is a consumerist demand and also a lucrative opportunity for established corporate wealth to mop up new markets and to collect government moneys in green new deals perhaps. A greening of the status quo is a revolution of sorts, but it does not solve our problem, which is the status quo itself. Our revolution must be firstly against ourselves – our ways of life – our own status quo, then secondly against obstacles to that transformation – corporate monopoly, status monopoly, money monopoly, information monopoly and the consenting politics, which props up and enables all those things.

One small thing – Greta Thunberg advises us to follow the science – she means of climate change. I love Greta, but she should be very careful in scientific company. Science does not mean truth. I think the peer review system is now so rotten, so interconnected with career prospects, university guidelines, funding complications, commerce and power, that I think it can also mean a very large dose of delusion and careerist lies. The science on "our" side of the argument can be equally suspect. Just as Albert Einstein returned to Newton to test relativity, so we must return to solid ground; to trial and error; to our own experience, to test the latest scientific papers. The value of science is its detachment from both pre-conception and post-conception. It lets new light into personal per-ception of things, but it cannot instruct us how to act. That is for skill, dexterity, pragmatism – for trades' people to decide, perhaps using that new scientific illumination, but combined with old understanding and the perennial moral of what it means to be human.

W B Yeats sang, and so should we.

> Irish poets, learn your trade – sing whatever is well made – scorn the sort now growing up – all out of shape from toe to top – their un-remembering hearts and heads – base products of base beds.

If we are not rooted in our trades and culturing, we have nothing to give. When the trades rise up against the monopolies, then we can have a true rebellion. When baker, weaver, carpenter, farmer, sailor, brewer, stone mason, forester... rise up by methods which thrive without oil and biofuels (without fire, or very limited fire) then we can truly have the revolution, which the children ask of us. Culture is not what we demand, but what we do. Much of our now terrible predicament has been caused by monopoly – by unskilled "professional people" – by architects instructing and distorting the skills of builders, by "research bodies", or pesticide manufacturers instructing and distorting the skills of farmers, by peer-reviewed ignorance instructing and distorting us all.

So, our revolt is an ancient one – against the enclosures. Why do we revolt? – for love and gratitude - for the gift of life and for our children, parents, friends, neighbours – and for the near infinite variety of interconnected dependencies of awesome species for awesome species - and for the knowledge we can have at our finger tips, which those in power have lost.

****

CHAPTER 8 – DE-SCHOOLING SOCIETY

Yes. When the trades rise up against the monopolies, then we can have the true rebellion. When intelligence, ingenuity, dexterity and probity throw off the stifling and wealth-extracting "guidance" of research institutes, consultants, architects – the whole education industry, which is designed to extract rent in exchange for a subservience, which will continue to doff its cap without grudge.

That "guidance" has brought us rising sea levels, catastrophic decline of both biomass and biodiversity, empty holes in the ground where resources once lay, wildly increasing poverty for most and wildly increasing wealth for a few. It guides us to an iceless arctic, terrible storms, drought and extreme rainfall – to cascading soil life and famine.

Education has achieved all this, yet people facing a particular problem, will still say, what we need is education. What backward people need is education – what deprived areas need is education – what entrapped women need is education – what climate change deniers need is education.

A result of education has been to overlie and diminish sensual intelligence and specifically: immediate, pragmatic, and personal intelligence of our surroundings; of the effects of what we do as trades' people; of the evidence of our own senses. And so, information particular to our terrains and actions remains un-gathered for larger society. I see educated doctrine as the senseless leading the de-sensed.

It is plain that education has brought what we know as civilisation to an end and is about to cause unthinkable tragedy. Yet still we say, how can we educate people to behave better?

The problem is education. People have been educated into the enclosures – either into the rent gathering monopolies of the "professions", or otherwise into limp acceptance of a failure to ascend to professional status. (Status enclosure.)

Let's step outside the educated noise (truly, senseless noise) and just listen.

Let's listen for a while to Ivan Illich addressing Peace Corps students in Cuernavaca – it could equally have been to VSO volunteers.

> *It is incredibly unfair for you to impose yourselves on a village where you are so linguistically deaf and dumb that you don't even understand what you are doing, or what people think of you. And it is profoundly damaging to yourselves when you define something that you want to do as "good," a "sacrifice" and "help."*
>
> *I am here to suggest that you voluntarily renounce exercising the power which being an American gives you. I am here to entreat you to freely, consciously and humbly give up the legal right you have to impose your benevolence on Mexico. I am here to challenge you to recognize your inability, your powerlessness and your incapacity to do the "good" which you intended to do.*
>
> *I am here to entreat you to use your money, your status and your education to travel in Latin America. Come to look, come to climb our mountains, to enjoy our flowers. Come to study. But do not come to help.*

Full text here:
http://www.davidtinapple.com/illich/1968_cuernavaca.html

Or here is Gerrard Winstanley –

> *...a studying imagination comes into man, which is the devil for it is the cause of all evil, and sorrows in the World; that is he who puts out the eyes of man's Knowledge and tells him he must believe what others have writ or spoke, and not trust his own experience.*

We have been educated into a crazy phantasy, which has made sensual evidence redundant.

We pay crippling rents to GPs, solicitors, dentists, architects, planning consultants – consultants of all kinds and we watch as our trades decay and as our means to social pleasures disappear.

Farmers read instructions on the latest drums and sacks. They've no idea what's in the drums and sacks, but since they are the latest, they look up to proudly declare "I'm the cutting edge of industry." Sadly, she believes what others have writ or spoke and does not trust her own experience.

Status enclosure has no mention in the commons/enclosure literature, yet I think it pernicious as any of the others – land property, money property, thought property...

If we are to "build a society, in which work and pleasure are within walking distance from everyone's door", then we must see that both education and status enclosure are major obstacles to that end. We will need to urgently regain the evidence of our senses. Fortunately, that is also a road to happiness.

Change must come so rapidly that the unexpected will be everywhere. Doctrine will not sense it. For that we need our own senses, combined with sympathy, empathy.

And we'll need resolve in the face of tragedy. There is no path from here to happiness that can avoid tragedy. As we shall see in the next chapter, we must accept a very dark chaos and plunge right in.

****

CHAPTER 9 – CHOOSING TRAGEDY

Previously, we had chosen the bonny road and so we must, but that road also leads under the hill through good and evil; through an over-dose of truth. We've also explored the problems of de-growth, while using GDP as a measure – as though we could degrow to an optimum point without consequence. We cannot. De-growth will have terrible consequence. We cannot but pass though that terror. We must endure it.

The current casino of currency manipulation, usury and advantageous/disadvantageous roulette wheels of stocks, bonds, shares and futures, will crash without growth – that is: without the hopes of punters. That is how the casino spins – not by reason, but by the faith and dreams of punters. Once that faith and the possibility (the odds) of dreaming shatter, then the whole casino shatters.

Plainly the casino is so destructive that we must somehow remove it. But I say, we cannot remove it without tragedy. So it is that we must choose tragedy and pass through it, if we are to reach the other side of the hill.

The casino and the real economy of households, work-places and pleasures are too entwined to separate without pain. Yet, we must somehow remove the casino, so that the economy can function properly in its terrain again. I say, again, because the remedies we have, live in our cultural histories – awaiting adaption to the times.

As the casino shrinks (degrows) towards its terminal cascade, so companies will fold, unemployment will soar, tax revenue will wither and social infrastructures will wither accordingly. That means people will be without both wages and unemployment relief. I leave the collapse of other social infrastructures to your imagination. It is very simple to understand. Let's hope we are brave enough to face its darkness.

If we do not choose such a tragedy, then the end will be far, far worse – the extinction, or near extinction of human life as we know it. That extinction is approaching faster than all educated models had predicted. I'll not make a prediction to add to the noise, but I know this, unless I change instantly, to a life without oil, it will prove too late. That is the only truth.

As the casino collapses – as banks, employment and other means to a living collapse, there will remain an underlying miracle. The physical world will remain untouched – soils, crops, water, fungi, plants and animals - new possibilities for trade and the trades – all will remain in their physics. Human casino fantasy will also remain and human obstacles to that physics will remain to be overcome, but nevertheless all that can be physically sensed will be just as apparent as before the collapse.

So, we return to our theme that both work and pleasure must be walking distance from everyone's door. If we can build such connections by reviving population centres of towns and villages – by supporting each other's trades, and by evacuating the trades of the casino, then we can, with a large dose of luck, provide real economic islands in the storm of the crashing casino.

It'll be a close-run thing, because those larger storms are fast-approaching, just as the lesser, but still terrible storms of collapsing casinos will be impeding much of what we try to do. We must de-school and de-educate ourselves and listen to the new evidence of our senses and of each other. Look into the eyes of children. Feed on the skills of your trade and delight in the skills of others. Beautiful music and literature are threaded through with tragedy. We can carry words and music in our hearts. Best foot forward. Stiff upper lip, old thing. Is that over the top? Well yes, precisely. Don't forget that comedy and tragedy share identical plots. Look at our lives. We are comic. We cannot but be comic. Comedy is a useful sheltering arm. I've quoted this from Patrick Kavanagh before: *"Tragedy is comedy not fully born."* We may as well add W B Yeats – *"a terrible beauty is born".*

****

CHAPTER 10 – MANIFESTO

Should I make a manifesto for a society in which work and pleasure are all within walking distances? That is, a society in which human-sized tools replace fossil-fuelled machinery and in which commons of perceptive good behaviour replace the imperceptive amorality of power's enclosures. Do I need a banner to mark where I stand? If I criticise the banners of others, then I must show where I stand, so that I too can be criticised.

Horticultural Society

I say that cultures must retreat and so let the wilds expand. Of course, hunter/gatherer cultures have integrated with the wild as one species among the rest, but that is a far-off dream for us – of paradise before the fall.

Although we cannot have a secure food supply, without also creating surplus to carry from good years to bad and between the scarcity/surplus of regions, we must grow food within as small a space as we can. That is, we must think of both time and space.

What is humanity's ration of soil? Thinking of rations is more helpful than thinking of limits. We shall explore that later.

What is humanity's ration of oil? We consumed it many years ago. We should think of it as zero, plus a large measure of shame. We cannot think of it as zero, plus dispensation for negative emissions. Only the wilds can "draw down carbon". That is why we must shrink our culture to just humanity's ration within the larger ecology.

Many, on the green side of arguments make large sequestration claims for a variety of growing systems (negative emissions). These views are often held with a passion, because they provide personal dispensation. With regards to fossil fuels, what's done is done – no dispensations, pardons, or indulgencies can remove that shame. In all cases, those negative emissions are a fiction.

45

Religions have existing frameworks for dealing with shame – stories of agriculture's Fall from God-given nature are almost universal. They are deeply embodied in cultural tradition – and have been repeated forever. Now, after thousands of years of repeated misbehaviour, we are faced with a final reckoning, which asks of us, and of atheists like me, just how far can we continue to fall?

We continue to fall too fast if we:

1. Fail to replace oil-sized tools, with human-sized tools.

2. Continue to replace natural systems with designed systems for the subjugation of nature, by fossil fuels, pesticides, fungicides, herbicides and artificial fertilisers.

3. Continue to claim false dispensation for our various niches through "organic", "permaculture", "vegan", "pasture-fed", "agroecology" and "agroforestry" virtue signals. None of those systems will "draw down carbon" further than an optimum point - although they can restore soil vitality to that optimum point of balance. Often, husbandry mistakes, combined with a naturally par-blind human understanding, will bring us to the wrong side of that balance. Nevertheless, organic and etc are the cyclic systems we must follow, but accompanied by less hubris and more uncertainty.

4. Continue to disconnect elements of agricultural economy. A field, a town and a monetary system are all parts of the same whole. Organic, permacultural and agro-ecological organisations, have all been guilty (and dangerously so) of that disconnection. For instance, we find organically-grown produce in super markets, retail parks and internet-based box schemes. How can that be?

5. Continue to think that we can escape the fall. Agriculture is the fall. We can go a long way to diminishing its ill effects, but never entirely. For atmospheric stability, we must depend on the complex efficiencies of the wilds, while shrinking cultural footprints as much as we can – That is, a shrinkage towards our central goal – a society in which both work and pleasure are within walking distances, in which husbandry becomes human-sized (horticulture) and

in which energies of tide, sun, wind and gravity propel a far less powerful culture. We must do without much that fossil fuels and biofuels have provided. They cannot be replaced. We must quench nearly all our fires.

While accepting that hunter-gatherer cultures provide the true lesson, large-population agricultures can only continue indefinitely by:

1. Integrating with the wider ecology as much as they can.

2. Accepting a limited agricultural ration of that larger ecology, in which husbandry is observant, quick to adapt and efficient. Optimum crop yield from an allotted volume of soil and water must be accepted as a moral necessity. In that way, human-controlled acreage can be reduced, so that the wilds can expand. We must accept this moral statement - Only the wilds can draw down further carbon. Good husbandry can only aim for balance, while accepting that it will often fall short of that balance.

3. That means a change from an agricultural to a horticultural mindset, in which large numbers of people with human-sized tools, replace the prevailing and now impossible mindset of very small numbers of people with very large and powerful tools. That greater number of people, also means a greater capacity for perception, ingenuity and quick adaption.

4. Arrange for work and pleasure to sit within walking distances, by re-centring suburbia, into towns and villages interspersed with productive fields, gardens and orchards and by reviving the ancient home of trade and the trades and also of pleasures – existing towns and villages.

Without fossil fuels and biofuels, we shall have no energy to spare for transport. Wind, solar, hydro and tidal powers will prove sufficient, only for domestic and commercial heat, light, refrigeration and cookery. Don't forget that such a demand will more than double – perhaps triple, current electricity demand – even though we live more frugal and less demanding lives.

Of course, wind will provide truly-renewable power for sail-trade and similarly, wind, tide and water (gravity) can provide truly

47

renewable power for direct traction of pumps, mills and manufactories.

Once upon a time, every large town and city was built on a shore line, estuary, or navigable river. The early industrial revolution solved the inland problem by building canals. Those structures, though decayed await revival. Not only by canal and river, trade has also been by shore-hopping between small harbours along every mile of coastline. Can we have the electric railway? I may be wrong, but I think not. Electricity will have many more essential demands – principally heat and cookery.

****

This manifesto will prove schismatic to most, because it proposes that bio-fuels contribute far more to climate heating than fossil fuels. It says that they diminish both biomass and biodiversity, while also massively reducing the power of photosynthesis to "draw down carbon". I include the innocent-sounding domestic log burner, or wood-chip boiler in my list of evils!

It follows that for ceramics and metal working (or rather, reworking) it would be better to use coal, gas, or oil than both timber and charcoal. Such uses for fossil resources would leave biomass and diversity to live and breathe, but would also require the use of yet untried carbon capture and storage. CCS would, in any case, be needed for biomass, or charcoal burning. CCS has provided the great excuse for those wishing to continue the current (suicidal) status quo, so I present the possibility with diffidence and with insufficient knowledge. It remains true that burning coal with effective CCS would be far less destructive than burning timber with effective CCS.

There is one exception to the biomass rule – that is anaerobic digestion of wastes to produce useful methane, while also returning biomass "digestate" to the soil. The burning of methane emits carbon dioxide, but the digestate grows compensatory photosynthetic biomass. I don't know if anaerobic digestion will end the right, or wrong side of a carbon balance. But consider this – fermentation of some kind must happen anyway – in soil, or out of soil – plants need the simple minerals, which fermentation provides. I suspect a balance depends on both efficiencies of production and efficiencies of agricultural return. Certainly, we cannot dedicate

48

crops for gas production, since our difficulty is to grow enough food on as small an acreage as we can. Gas production can be used as an alternative to aerobic composting of wastes - not as an end in itself. It may prove valuable, on a small scale, for domestic cookery, or heat.

Grassland and animals.

Even though ruminants convert grass that people cannot eat, into food that they can and even though well-managed grassland can undoubtedly prove to be a more, or less balanced system, nevertheless the acreage will be too extensive. Such a system cannot "draw down carbon" beyond an optimum point, as many proponents suggest. Such grassland will be better used for re-foresting, or re-wilding – that is for photosynthesis, biomass, biodiversity and some timber production. Communities will have a greater need for timber than for meat. Such a reversion may also provide the settlement of an ancient social injustice – that is a return of the commons from the vicious enclosures of past centuries, which turned people from the land, in return for the wealth of a few in the golden fleece. Woodland provides more employment than sheep ever could.

Even so, grassland as green manure in crop rotation is ancient and effective. Animals for milk, meat and eggs, can add to, rather than diminish crop rotation. They do not increase the horticultural acreage. Rather, they diminish the considerable energy needed for cutting and mulching the same acreage of green manure. Green manure will prove essential for a regenerative agriculture and animals are an energy-efficient way to use it. Don't forget that horticultural acreage will include cereals and the considerable manual labour involved. Will we have the energy for regular cutting and mulching of green manure? – I suspect "dog and stick" will prove a welcome physical and dietary relief. In a ratio of two acres of green manure to one of cropping, we can still have eggs, milk and meat – but rationed for feast days, weekends and holidays.

With regards to the new wild, which we hope will re-find its evolutionary balance of plant to animal, hunter-gatherer codes of good behaviour may guide a new and rationed supply of wild meat for settled communities.

I think a weakness in vegan agriculture is that it ignores the lessons of that evolutionary balance. Even so, I respect vegan goals to tread lightly and vegan crop rotations are valuable lessons in similarly treading lightly. Those vegan goals have made us think more productively about perennial systems – beyond orchards and nut trees, we can also consider perennial cereals (the Land Institute). Considering perennial cereal cropping, we'd also have to think (paradoxically) of rotation. Since we'd remove both seed and straw, a harvest would remove a lot of soil vitality. We'd still need that two to one ratio - and again, grazing would provide a productive respite from the scythe – not that the scythe is an unpleasant tool – in good company on a sunny day.

Commons, or enclosure. Rations, or limits.

Let's consider this – Enlightened, peer-reviewed education has brought us to a cliff edge of utter catastrophe – the end of human cultures as we've known them and the extinction of very many species, which have accompanied our common evolution to this point. Yet still, people will declare, "What we need is education" to educate farmers, builders, fishermen, climate change deniers... Listen to the science! say campaigners.

Yet, it is plain that education has taught farmers the efficacy of pesticides, fungicides, herbicides... and has made the educators rich and both farmers and their lands, very much poorer.

Only a handful of farmers have survived that educated, peer-reviewed invasion and they continue to disappear.

Architects have replaced the functional, elegant and appropriate work of builders, with inappropriate, ugly, but educated design. In the process architects have become rich and builders, poor. (I do not speak of builders who have become rich by idle accumulation of land value). Is there a single architectural design that can match the beauty of a simple parish church – or almost any house before the seventeenth century? Almost no beauty and none of the ingenuity, dexterity and deep understanding of a builder, for her terrain and her materials has survived the manipulation and rent-gathering of architects.

In short, the real economy of households and the trades has been bled dry by education. Enclosed professions demand terrible rents for their professional status. GPs, solicitors, architects and consultants of all kinds will commonly demand £300 per hour from the ordinary wage of someone who earns £10 per hour.

Status enclosure, money enclosure (interest is rent), land enclosure and intellectual property enclosure will eventually bring any economy to its knees. Educated opinion has created the idea of austerity, so that remaining money-flow can remain in those same hands.

Anyone, who writes of stories such as this, will be asked for peer-reviewed sources from within that same rent gathering, educational system.

Here's a thing - There are many fine permaculture practitioners. But we must beware of permaculture designers. They are educators extracting rent. Let them emerge from the enclosures to become practitioners – otherwise they may inflict the same old educational harm.

Thinking of species extinction and climate heating, almost all influential ideas – that is, those accepted by news sources, governments, politicians and NGOs, come from the peer-reviewed, or rather, career-reviewed people of educated status. That status has no senses – it is truly senseless. Of course, true science must remain sceptical and outside moral preconception. It can have no application, because every act has consequence and every consequence must have a moral. Sadly, I see little evidence of that true science, although, of course it has survived as history has always depicted – not in shiny laboratories, or hallowed halls, but in dusty attics. Meanwhile, leaving true science to her studies, it is up to those who act, to morally decide what to do. The pragmatic ingenuity of a trades' person may be curious for the science, but nevertheless, it is the trades' person who must decide how to act. Of course, any householder is in that same position.

This manifesto calls for householders and trades' people of every kind to shrug off the enclosures and to apply the love, skill and ingenuities that only they can find. We cannot "improve" the enclosures. We must abandon them and if we can, step back onto the common. We have very little time.

Enclosures have limits – thin lines within which behaviour can be as we choose. Soil, resources and bad behaviour can remain undefined within them. Trespassers will be prosecuted.

The common has rations – of both time and space – of what we can do and of where and how we can stand. A ration can be loved and shared – it has qualities – tastes, touch, scents, sights and sounds – it is distributed in fair shares of both chores and pleasures. It is received from ancestors and must be bequeathed to descendants. Such commons survive in the household, where they are easily understood. I behave by a filial code. But in the work place they are lost. This manifesto is largely a call for their revival. If we can behave well in the household, then we can also do so at work. A culture is what people do, not who they are, or claim to be.

Population.

I will not speak of population statistics. Overpopulation is here and now, just as and because of our wild use of fossil fuels. There are no remedies, but to leave fossil fuels in the ground and to personally consider the need to bring more babies into an over-crowded world. I will not engage with those who use over-population as a means to ridicule attempts to find ways to integrate cultures into the ecologies which must sustain them. The currently tragic effects of both fossil fuels and too many people are what they are. What's done is done. We must endure them, while living differently and so not adding to those problems. The present creates the future. Our present of over-population, species extinction and catastrophic climate heating was created by the past – including our personal pasts. We cannot change the past, but we can change the future. That may seem obvious, but studying social polemics, plainly it is not. That it is unlikely we can reverse catastrophic climate heating, does not make attempts invalid. Rather, it makes the attempt, romantic, beautiful, egalitarian and essential to even a temporal happiness. Mention of sail-trade and the scythe will attract ridicule from nearly every green and educated NGO, and yet truly, there is no other way. The educated must be ignored, or more hopefully, de-schooled, to be re-awakened to the soil, sun, wind and rain and also to true happiness.

****

CHAPTER 11 – SOVEREINGTY

It's a fine thing, we say, to take back control of our seeds, our food production and our lives. It's plain that consumerism has brought us to a cliff edge. Ordinary people must gain sovereignty over methods of production, because dependency on the sovereignty of others had brought chaos. We have not been acting on the evidence of our senses, instead we have been lobbying that others – our providers - act on that evidence. We pay for the produce and ask for it to be just as we like. That is the consumerist contract.

Many in Extinction Rebellion are asking just that – that governments and corporations change their provisions to be just as they'd like. It may be that the bulk of people in the protests form a consumerist rebellion. The UK Green Party and the "educated" middle class are at the heart of that dependant outcry.

They demand the better behaviour of banks, oil companies and governments. Prominent journalists have made sure that they have been very publicly arrested. The one demand they do not make is to take back sovereignty. Unlike true commons movements, such as the diggers, who simply, elegantly and truthfully dug, they demand nothing more than the changed behaviour of existing monopolies.

Yet, if people did not buy oil, oil companies would evaporate. If people did not fly, no aeroplanes could take off. Such a movement would be in the commons-tradition. That tradition remains in our intrinsic morality. It is easily understood and could be inspirational. If we all shopped at market stalls, or the proper shops of skilled trades' people, then the super market would close. Sovereignty of skill and ingenuity could be returned to the commons and life would return to our half-dead towns and villages.

If the Extinction Rebellion was rebellion against ourselves and our current ways of life, then it would prove a true rebellion. I've seen little evidence of that.

The School Strike for Climate asks that adults take control of their lives, their trades and their work-places – and that they begin to behave properly as adults should. It could have provided the spur to a real commons/real economic movement. Instead, we adults have cleverly betrayed the earnest eyes of children and have shrugged responsibility from ourselves to the abstract shoulders of an abstract idea – a government; a corporation. Extinction Rebellion has betrayed the School Strike, to fight what does not exist – only people and their resources exist. A corporation is an abstract idea, made physical by the very many purchases, which we ordinary adults make. To truly see the fabric of a corporation, watch a que at a super-market check-out, or count the clicks on their web sites. Viva School Strike! - but it seems to me that Extinction Rebellion, remains locked in consumerism. It expresses the outrage of the green consumer. Already corporations are re-writing mission statements to include those new "green" markets. If it's the coming thing, then it's theirs to be exploited. Does Extinction Rebellion ask for that exploitation? – Plainly, yes, since it asks for those corporate/government changes.

But then again, some may demand sovereignty without caring what they'd have sovereignty over and how – my life? your seeds? Do they ask for a simple transference of power from old vices to a new, but ill-defined virtue? If I have a skill, then it is natural to want sovereignty over my workshop, my farm, my mill, or my potter's wheel. What we do creates the culture and what we do is specific. But undefined sovereignty is dangerous. It creates a new enclosure.

Every little sovereign, over every little field, or baker's oven must be bound by the greater law – the law of the commons. Over centuries, commons have been broken and scattered in the spoil heaps of enclosure. In an enclosure, my field, or my work-place becomes my sovereign castle, in which I can behave as badly as I choose, and in which no trespassers may be lawfully permitted to say otherwise.

Here is the true rebellion – as the children say – of ancestors and descendants, embodied in contemporary behaviour. As the children also say, behave! By all that's holy, dig like a leveller! Sing the joy of the ol' sun 'n moon illuminating a durable, responsive culturing of our mothering soil. And they say, be kind.

****

CHAPTER 12 – ISLANDS IN THE FLOOD

This is expanded from a conversation with my virtual friend Michelle Galimba about the pleasures we find in necessary hiding places from the truth. Michelle writes with a beautifully clear eye. *https://www.animasoul.org/2019/10/20/the-speech/*

You'll often find me hiding in the shade; in refuges from the truth, and our own farm is a long way off course – in its various hiding places. The loveliest refuge is the present - in companionship and pleasures - sights, sounds, scents... in little projects and jobs we have in hand – the sight of freshly weeded rows of vegetables, or newly-pruned orchard trees. But when I step from the timeless present to time again, the horror would overwhelm me, but for the utopian light, the other side of darkness. Utopia is not fanciful. Our lives are that. It is imaginative and true. Utopia is possible. It is our weakness which makes it apparently impossible. That leads to another journey - companionship in our common folly - in forgiveness, charity, comedy and tragedy. That journey is one of utopian compromise.

However, nearly all "green" and egalitarian solutions, which we find in places such as resilience.org are compromises, on the last debunked compromise. I'll not have that! I say, we must return to the original Utopia. That is, we compromise the beautiful and true.

Living in the timeless present, we find sensual evidence of the truth. That innocence is most receptive to the only true evidence – that is sensual evidence. Sensual evidence must always pass through the senses of someone. It is always solitary. But, when we contemplate our next footstep through that sensual landscape, we re-enter a world of time and consequence. We cannot remain innocent. Both future and past consequences intrude. We must judge. We step into a moral world. Whose morals? – mine, or yours? – mine, or the consensus, the law's, the elite's, the ancestors? Prudence, expediency, fear, anger, all intrude.

The academic title we have for the study of those moral questions is economics. Because uncovered moral truth is a danger to what we may call "the powers", economics is no longer studied in UK universities. Instead, the study has been narrowed to the limits of an accepted landscape – or rather, people-scape, of unchallenged enclosures and assumptions. In that people-scape, people who call themselves economists, study what remains inside an enclosure – rent and the necessary freedom of rent – that is the necessary amorality, which liberates what they call, the market. Enclosed mediums of exchange, become property, which generates rent (money interest), enclosed professions, become property which generates rent (lawyers, GPs, architects and so on). Enclosed land becomes property. Enclosed ideas become property.

In all those cases the near-infinitely complex physics of soil, fungi, bacteria, plants, animals, forests, rivers, people... are excluded from study to be replaced by the simplicity of amorality and rent. Because people pay rent for something which does not exist (property is an idea), it is thought that an "economy" can sustain infinite growth and defy the indisputably finite nature of labour, resource and the land.

Everywhere, good housekeepers understand that finity. It is apparent through every sense – taste, touch, sound, sight. It must be prudently managed and wisely shared. A good housekeeper must follow, or learn codes of behaviour, by distribution of fair shares of what we can have and what we can do, in food, clothing, toys, chores and pleasures. That is, she must regulate both what her family does and what it can have. She must budget today's income for the days ahead. In short, she must study economics. Readers will know that a housekeeper and an economist in the same sentence make a tautology.

So, as Brian Davey notes, there can be no conversation between a householding economist and an "economist" of the enclosures – or between ordinary pragmatism and university guide-lines, peer-reviews, or career reviews (another tautology). *http://www.feasta.org/2019/10/03/the-school-of-economics-as-a-suicide-academy/*

All enclosures have been first achieved by violence. Their powers are then extended by rent. The fence lines, become castellated by law and by peer-review/career review. Schools and universities further consolidate an enclosed future by education.

Without increasing spending (GDP) there can be no rent. Fellow real economic writers would say debt, but it is not only debt. It is wider – it is rent. Money as property is not the only enclosure demanding rent. A world of enclosures will collapse without expanding GDP. University "economists" almost exclusively focus on rent/debt and the maintenance of perpetually expanding spending. Any child can see that such economists have no clothes. Plainly, children must be swiftly educated to imagine them dressed again. Professional monopolies of law, bank, medicine, pharmaceuticals, architecture and so on, utterly depend on the educated illusion. Otherwise they'd lose the means to charge such fabulous rents for their professional status. An ordinary householder would no longer be compelled to pay a rent of £300 per hour, from her own wage of £10 per hour. That £290 per hour can only exist by the means of fantasy money - casino money - true economy bleeding money. Even university economists, who calculate, only the odds of a casino, can see that the world of real resource and real labour is incapable, on its own, of paying such massive rents. For that, money flow must accelerate and GDP (spending) must expand.

A so called, steady state economy, or a circular economy, also means the end of professional monopoly and the end of rent. Money flow must shadow the transformative power of what people can do, which means it is limited to just that – with none to spare for the fantasies of enclosed monopoly. This author, who has no career review, thinks that the end of growth means the total collapse of the casino. Though that collapse will bring havoc to most people's lives, he cannot see a way forward, but to first pass through the tragedy to gain the light on the other side. What's done is done. The currently massive money-flow hovers above a much shrunken and mismatched energy-flow and will in any case implode, sometime soon. He has no Chrystal ball, but until it does implode, it gives time to build islands of a real economy which can emerge more or less intact from beneath the smoke and embers. After all, it is a fantasy, which will have collapsed – a gamblers dream. The physics of the world – people, fields, woods, rivers – will all remain.

57

We return to the ancient conflict between commons and enclosure and to a sentence which my virtual friend Michelle singled out - *But when I step from the timeless present to time again, the horror would overwhelm me, but for the utopian light, the other side of darkness.*

Yes – the loveliest refuge from the horror to come, is the timeless present – in companionship, fields, woods and so on, but also in work and companionship of work – each to her skill, to build living islands, which may survive collapsing casinos, rising seas and violently defensive enclosures. From time to time though, we must step back into time with a steady eye for both the Utopia ahead and the tragedy, which surrounds us.

****

CHAPTER 13 – POLITICS

While busy building real economic islands on the common, we will be hindered by the contrary powers of enclosure – so we must also engage with those powers.

In that engagement we mustn't forget that our primary purpose is to rebuild the common. Soon, both common and enclosure will be swept into chaos by collapsing ecologies, storms and rising seas – and of course, by collapsing monetary systems. Only the utterly changed personal behaviours of everyone can prevent what is after all – doomsday. It is not true, as most people say, that one person can do nothing. We have come to a unique moment, when only the actions of everyone – one by one, can pause our crazy trajectory over the brink. Governments have not the power.

Is my personal behaviour utterly changed? It is not. So, I begin, not with the "grief" that rather narcissistic "climate activists" claim, but with deep, nearly overwhelming shame.

Of course, we are a clan-forming, flocking species. Our identities are tied to others and our roles are integral to other roles. So, personal change becomes much more difficult - but also, more effective, because it ripples through the larger clan of family, friends and work-places. How else do social fashions spread so quickly?

No! You say they are spread by television and popular newspapers – political and otherwise and by the subversive power of political propaganda and commercial advertising. You are right – in a world of enclosure, but you are also wrong - we are descending to the real world of the common.

In a world of enclosures; in the ballot and in the market-place, we can choose least worst options and on rare occasions, those which are good. For the most part, we choose those which do least harm.

Let's return to our theme – a society, in which both work and pleasure are walking distances from everyone's door. In the currently overwhelming world of political, journalistic and commercial enclosures, how do we ease small roads of exodus towards that hopefully attractive common?

Never ever fly. That is easy.

If we can, we should no longer shop in super markets, but instead find proper trade's people and market stalls. Find people.

Learn human-sized technologies and shed those powered by coal, gas, oil and biofuels. Such technologies need the intelligence, ingenuity and dexterity of very many people, not the blind dependencies of oil. So, again, find people.

Vote for the least-worst political party.

Here in the UK, that choice is so obvious and so viciously opposed by monopolies of every kind, that it is very odd to have to mention it. The Labour Party is still tainted by its electorally-successful, corporate-backed departure into monetarism and war, but nevertheless the almost miraculous rise of Jeremy Corbyn and his supporters – the ghosts of Clement Atlee - should be embraced by all our hearts and minds as the miracle it is – an ordinary, incorruptible, egalitarian, green, moderate politician, somehow and against all odds, close to "the seat of power"!

In the UK there are two political parties with similar policies, to those of Jeremy Corbyn's Labour – Plaid Cymru (The Party of Wales) and the Green Party.

The Scottish National Party is close to Plaid, Green and Labour, but is tainted by love for Scottish oil. We cannot avoid such taints in politics – The Green Party is similarly tainted by its love for statutory consumer-rights, exchanged for protected corporate supply, embodied by European Economic Union. Since the same contract also exists inside Westminster, Plaid Cymru (and SNP) have more legitimate claims (to the Greens) to remain in the Economic Union by seeking national independence.

Of course, corporate/media-backed, old/New Labour politicians are a threat to the integrity of the Labour Party, even so it remains the only party to have a chance for power in Westminster. We should embrace it.

There you have it, an innocent's guide to power in politics.

Don't knock innocence.

****

CHAPTER 14 – UTOPIA IS THE LAST REMAINING REALISM

We can find sufficient solar, hydro & wind energy for the current needs of the electricity grid, but for the new needs of domestic and commercial heat and of manufacturing (ceramics, smelting...) - we've not a hope in hell unless we dramatically reduce demands to at least a tenth. Transport, either electric, or hydrogen? - impossible. Renewable systems have not the capacity. Hydrogen is not a source of energy. It is a means to store surplus electrical energy.

Meanwhile, any further use of either fossil fuel, or biofuel means climatic suicide. We neglected to apply planned descents from fossil-burning ways of life, many decades ago. Today is too late. We must instantly quench the fires. Impossible? - Yes. But, since we have squandered all others, the impossible remains our only choice.

So, what do we have? – the return of personal intelligence, ingenuity & dexterity - people-sized technology - agriculture integrated with its ecology, sail-trade, river & canal trade, vibrant towns & villages, sizzling with revived skills of the trades – all within walking distances. Renaissance.

Utopian renaissance is the only choice remaining - Choose it, or we choose the end of human cultures. It is simple.

Governments have not the power to make such changes. Only immediate reclamation of dynamic commons from the static powers of the enclosures can liberate renaissance.

These tax-generated cultural commons, though often decayed, remain in place – roads, streets, bridges, harbours, canals, navigable rivers, weirs, market squares and halls, libraries, concert halls, theatres, playing fields, parks, allotments, sewage systems, flood defences, sluices, drainage, lakes and reservoirs, hospitals, electrical grids and water supplies, monetary systems, town halls and parliament buildings... These are all basically communistic systems – financed by the commons, which recent UK governments have sought to enclose into private hands. Of course, some canals, harbours and so on and also theatres, cinemas..., were built by private finance, but today their maintenance has usually returned to the common. To change that, means enclosure (privatisation) and rent.

People as tax payers and citizens have ancestral right to manage them on the common. Current enclosures bleed commonwealth into private hands. By rent, they shrink the common good, by increasing private good and without returning obligation.

Then, we have Earth Commons, which no one made and from which we receive all that we have – soils, seas, rivers and biomass – gifts which, if we live within their laws, will be self-renewing.

We also have minerals, fossils and salts, which do not remain in their original state if we use them – the original state is gone forever.

This is the case for burnt fossils, agricultural minerals and salts and aggregate for construction. We now have a disbalancing surplus of gas and energy produced by fire and chemical reaction (fossil engines, artificial fertilisers, cement making...) and a deficit of biomass (critical) and mineral mass (less critical).

Yes. We have a massive deficit of what we may call "cyclic nature" and a massive surplus of dangerous and linear human effects.

The current UK general election has thrown a selection of artificial choices before us all, so that we must choose one artifice from the rest. No party stands on the premise that Utopia is the last remaining realism, or that societies must arrange that work and pleasure are within the walking distance of every citizen. Yet, choosing one party or the other will have a profound difference on our singular abilities to reclaim the common and to reclaim those ends.

The current UK government's entire motivation has been to enclose the last commons into the private hands of a small elite. Some other parties have become entranced by the seeming enlightenment of the European Economic Union – even though it is founded on enclosures and monopolies and the complacent dependency of consumerism. Both those neo-liberal impulses are towards ecological destruction and climatic catastrophe.

Jeremy Corbyn's Labour Party has become the only political choice for Westminster. It (or Jeremy) can do nothing for us, but it may allow space to personally act – in time instantly – in space, shrinking till we fit our personal allotment of this lovely Earth.

Given that all other reasonings are now too late, give me one reason not to choose Utopia?

THE SERIOUSNESS OF CAREER REVIEW

Since my teenage years I've retained the following unshakeable certainty: that seriousness is an attitude we adopt, when we have a need to remove thought.

I think that other species can summon it too – for the posturing of rival males, for instance.

Politicians, gang leaders, career-chasers, journalists... all summon seriousness to increase the size of their posturing and to remove doubt.

We cannot argue with someone in a serious state, because they will have no means to find a thought in response. Only someone with a larger seriousness to their own can draw their attention.

There is a tragic irony, in that those we most look to for the quality of their thinking, are often most adept at subjugating thought. The worlds of art and science are almost rigid with thoughtlessness. Schools of thought draw themselves up in dignity, clear their collective throats and then also clear the decks of unruly intelligence – ready for action. Here is the school and there is the schism. Clearly anyone seeking an art, or science career must be schooled to thoughtlessness. Otherwise, they may fall into schism.

This has become so extreme in recent times that once-useful peer-review has mutated to the far simpler and more direct concept of career-review. Professions have become enclosed monopolies, who's central purpose is not to profess, but to show discretion – otherwise we are seen as unprofessional. For a discrete professional advice within closed walls, we must pay rent.

For myself, I no longer trust serious (of course thoughtless) papers on ecology, climate heating, economy, soil science... Nor do I trust a word of the string of IPCC reports – every one of which has used models, which have been wildly off the mark (optimistic) on sequestration, life-cycles, photosynthesis and CO_2 emissions. Every model has been disproved by subsequent events and every model has been far too kind to the status quo of politics and power.

Many, wait for new, revised models to guide their practical actions. They'd do better to let the seriousness evaporate and for the whole human creature to return. We have sensual evidence, which is unavailable to the serious. We have pragmatism, intelligence, companionship, joy and grief.

Look at this mass of burning coal and then at this same mass of burning forest – both of which are burnt for energy. Ah look – the CO_2 released from both is more or less the same and the energy gained also.

IPCC consensus warms its hands and professes – The tree is renewable. The tree is good. Another tree will grow. Coal is not renewable. It is bad. IPCC pronounces timber burning to be carbon neutral, because after thirty years the tree will photosynthesis again at a similar rate. IPCC is serious!

Any ordinary person with sensual intelligence can see that the IPCC is talking nonsense. Yet nearly all defer, because surely IPCC must be in possession of an esoteric knowledge to which they cannot ascend?

The truth about biomass burning is pragmatic. It is not esoteric. Neither is IPCC judgement scientific – not remotely. It is merely serious.

Firstly, where has all that lack of photosynthesis gone in those thirty years – certainly not into IPCC's ledger and certainly not into soil, into re-growth and into the species dependant on that tree.

Now, let's burn the coal, but not the tree – allowing it to grow leaves, shed leaves, increase in both soil and plant biomass and photosynthesis. Which is the better, burning coal, or burning trees? The answer is plain.

We must stop burning coal, but burning trees is far, far worse. Biomass burning removes life from the soil (sequestration), oxygen from the air and removes future photosynthetic effects. It follows that had we time for a planned transition towards atmospheric balance, then first we'd stop burning life, then second, we'd stop burning fossilised life.

Of course, we have no more time and all must be instant.

Biomass burning from land which has not changed its use – arable - oil-seeds, sugar cane, wheat, maize … and from existing forests is accounted zero carbon in all IPCC reports.

How on Earth did the scientific consensus come to believe (I think belief is appropriate) in nonsense? It can only be because it is serious and serious about protecting a doctrine - a doctrine which is tied to careers and to peer-reviews/career-reviews in their hundreds of thousands. Don't forget that climate-related "scientists" will wildly jet from global conference to global conference in serious defence of their careers – fully aware of the harm they do, yet also in the certainty that the integrity of professional and discrete status must always come first. The august must not be embarrassed. *

****

Authors note – As a humble farmer, my thoughts have been refused by reputable organisations such as resilience.org , who ask for my "sources". That they are my own would seem to protect anyone else from ridicule, but nevertheless, it seems, I remain without appropriate peers.

CHAPTER 15 – THE COUP

The brutes are closing in and shutting down broadcasting, newspapers and what has remained of democracy. It is a coup, which has been gestating for an indeterminate time, but which has emerged into adulthood with extreme rapidity. In much of the world - particularly in both South and North America it has strutted for a while, but here in the UK, it has been quietly subversive until now, when the jackboots march through every TV channel, nearly all radio and every one of our mainstream newspapers. Of course, there are chinks of light, but those are for the most part quickly obscured by far the larger light-show of authorities, experts, pundits and TV breakfast sofa narcissists. In the shadows and backstreets some of us gather murmuring of better times.

To say it is a corporate coup would be inaccurate, but we can say that it is but a small group of men (mostly men) who are the so-called leaders of those corporations and whose source of fabulous wealth is sucked through those corporations. Spinning round the gold dusted light of the billionaires are widening rings of dancing acolytes - the millionaires; the power seekers; the mercenaries, not as moths to the flame, but as jackals around the kill of the pride.

Such is UK commerce today. Stand still and you can hear the sucking sound as the good soil beneath our feet, the minerals in the ground, the biomass of Earth, the balance of atmospheric gases. The tax-generated assets of roads, railways, canals, bridges, town halls, market squares, hospitals, libraries, government buildings are all drained upwards into the sequestering levitation of the coup.

A kind of capillary action lifts the rewards of skill, ingenuity and dexterities of millions into the vast hold of the super jet, neoliberalism, monetarism, militarism, rentism - no certainly not capitalism. Capitalism maintains capital.

Science fiction has materialised and materials (capital) are fast mutating into a planetary blanket of monetary soup. Soon, life will be too hot to handle and solid ground will be hard to find. How? – because we believe in fiction.

And here's a funny thing – instead of seeking solid ground and then living on it, while inviting others to join them there, people march in the street to persuade coup leaders to behave better. People want to be dependent on the coup and to remain in the pages of a fiction. Extinction Rebellion, Green Peace and the Green Party, spend all their time in a one-sided petition – a unilateral consumerist submission to the coup – we your dependents would like you to behave better, because we're worth it.

Meanwhile rivers, fields, woods . . .

That the coup could take control so easily inside the European Economic Union, is no accident. The EU is founded on the premise of benign corporate control, with built in consumer protections. The coup will be happy, inside, or outside the EU, to provide for whatever the people will spend. Forward thinking billionaires will happily green the coup, so long as the capillary is maintained. For all its professions on biodiversity and climate change the EU is contracted to maintain the capillary. Attempts at public ownership and assertions of a commonwealth will meet the full contrary forces of the EU, just as they'll meet the full contrary forces of the coup. Brexit, or Remain add drama to the fiction and the coup is happy to stir the passions of both camps. Divide and rule.

Expanding GDP and expanding CO_2 emissions are cause and effect. Consumerism is essential to both the EU and the coup. Neither can seek a steady state economy, because such an economy will generate no surplus to feed their parasitic intent.

Meanwhile, we cannot reduce emissions without shrinking our needs. Shrinking our needs will shrink the powers of both the EU and the coup. Shrinking to fit, just so, in our loved plot of Earth will deprive both EU and Coup of their life-blood – our spending. The jackboots may come to prevent us, but the sooner we make a start, so the sooner the thugs will lose strength to oppose us.

****

CHAPTER 16 – HEY HO, WE'RE BOUND FOR RIO

Since the Rio Earth Summit in 1992, man-made carbon emissions have risen steadily, dipping slightly in economic recession to resume as Gross World Product continues to expand.

The Intergovernmental Panel on Climate Change has achieved nothing. In truth, it has achieved almost universal complacency that something is being done at the highest level. Targets are very useful for the complacent. They mean we can change tomorrow – not today.

Meanwhile, democratically elected governments focus on expanding their Gross Domestic Products as a measure for the success of their governance. GDP and climate heating follow almost identical trajectories on a graph. They are cause and effect.

Today, for all the climate targets of the past, the moment has finally arrived – the terrible moment, when all targets have become too late. Action by governments, corporations and citizens, must be instant. Otherwise, humanity's brief four thousand years or so of agricultural settlements is certain to come to a horrible end. Readers may be surprised that modern cultures – cities, towns, roads and railways - are agricultures. They shouldn't be surprised.

Yet still, nearly everybody says - This is too big for me. I must lobby corporations and governments. I must earnestly study the latest IPCC document about how we might change tomorrow. Then I must mention it to my friends, while wisely casting my vote in the ballot.

Dear Everybody, it is too late for that. Faith in national and international institutions, commercial corporations and NGOs has pushed us to defer personal responsibility from ourselves to others.

Yet how do those others exist? – By ourselves – by our purchases, donations and democratic requests. In short, we pretended to buy redemption. Instead, we bought cascading ecologies on which we all depend and catastrophic climate heating. We created the monster. Now we attempt to negotiate with it. Instead, why not de-create it – stop the purchases, donations and democratic requests. Instead, we can buy and sell between ourselves – butcher, baker, candlestick maker… We can think for ourselves, rather than through the conduit of a favourite NGO. We can begin a new political process. Of course, all those actions can only be done in transition from one place to another. Even so, we must immediately make a start. We'll make mistakes, but mistakes are where new truth is revealed.

This is not too big for me. On the contrary, it is too big for governments, political parties, corporations and NGOs. We created all those things – those abstract ideas – and we created the physics of catastrophe. Abstractions such as governments and corporations can cause nothing, but through the physics of me. Yet our subscription-touting NGO send an endless flow of emails bosting of their expertise, requesting more money and saying not a word of our personal ways of life.

NGOs and political parties argue about targets. They speak of the future, but the future does not exist. All we can know of the future, is that it is created by the present. The present makes the future, whichever way we choose. Zero carbon by 2030, or 2045 is a distraction from our almost universal moral failure to act as the times demand – that is, immediately.

Unilateral action is all we have remaining. We can hope that others do the same, so that it becomes multilateral. But to negotiate multilateral agreement before we personally agree to act is suicide. Just as multilateral nuclear disarmament has led to the opposite, so it is on climate heating. The above is applicable to citizens, parishes, national governments and trade blocks, such as the EEU.

I find it tragic that nearly all my friends, just about every left-leaning, or "environment-leaning" NGO and even the UK Green Party prefer to lobby from a multilateral "position of strength". Strength itself is a problem, when every answer to the hubris of the times should be towards weakness – the utter dependence of the species on all the other species; the dependence of ourselves, on others. That essential new vision is also an old one, which is quite fitting for the flow of 1,500 years of UK cultures – has no one read of

70

Christianity? We don't need to be Christian to understand the truths it contains, or the ways it is woven into modern understanding. As an atheist myself, and one with a tendency to ancestor worship – the flow of inherited and bequeathed commons – I can also see that the best of Christianity (not the worst) has nurtured that flow – in sacred springs, local saints/ancestors – in the common follies of being human.

Such a common ethics can guide personal change, while at the same time stimulating multilateral change by a shear mass of people – accumulating one by one.

So-called, unilateral change works right through the system. Personal change becomes simpler, when we are disentangled from the lives of others. Parish changes become simpler, when it is disentangled from government restrictions and advise. Government change becomes simpler, when disentangled from international agreements. In other words, change can be far more rapid when we act alone and others act alone also. Of course, all those things are tangled anyway from personal to government entanglements – we are obliged, concerned, contracted... So, what do I mean?

This may seem to be high falutin' or deliberately obscure, but this is what I mean – To consider our next footstep, we consult inner moral commons and shrug off the obfuscation of the enclosures – the trade agreements and so on. Thus, we remain entangled at the deepest level, but are disentangled at the ephemeral level. That deep entanglement can be contagious, because everyone is a part.

If the UK government disarmed its nuclear arsenal, other governments would be more inclined to follow suit. It is a moral act and we all have morals.

If the UK government decided to act on climate change by (as it must to succeed) nationalising or severely regulating the adverse behaviours of corporations, banks and profligate citizens – and by creating avenues in which citizens could participate, then other governments would be more likely to follow suit.

We've seen how international climate agreements have led to increasing carbon emissions (the evidence is irrefutable). Less obvious to most, the EEU's introduction of negotiated environmental and consumer protections has, in the same way, led to increasing emissions, increasing corporate power and increasing consumer dependency on that power.

It is plain that to act quickly to limit environmental degradation and to reduce carbon emissions, UK must act independently of the EU, just as UK citizens must act independently of UK government. It is certain that the EU would vigorously oppose actions by its member states, which undermined its consumer/corporate contract by applying protectionist measures. In truth, any attempts to shrink national GDP, would also shrink the money flow of the Euro and so also the power of the EU. EU is obliged, by contract, to oppose the common good.

Remember, we seek weakness not power – by shrinking our effects into just a part of the whole of every species under the sun. We must learn to be fitting. No one can do that for us. How do we join the evolving flow of common humanity, while shrugging off the ephemeral madness of the times? For that, only my reader can know. The moral is universal, but the physics of life is specific in all its parts and is peculiar to every one of us in particular ways.

****

CHAPTER 17 – RITE OF PASSAGE

This year, the solstice is possibly a rite of passage, and possibly the end of days. The 21st and the 14th (UK election day) have merged in the imagination, just as rites of Christmas and the solstice are really one and the same.

The child of Spring may be born, or not. Humanity's pillage of nature is on that same, sharp fulcrum of time. It is the end of days, or it is rapid abandonment of much that we've thought normal – the family car, super markets, cheap food, aviation, suburbia, internet shopping, enclosed monopolies... If we emerge and the leaves return, then it must be to a society, in which "both work and pleasure are walking distance from everyone's door" – the theme of this book. Everyone must have a door and a fitting, contributory part in the whole.

This Winter is deep as it gets – the very depth of what it means to be human – personal intrinsic and filial morality, or not. Sing (and feel) holy, holy, holy, or wearily reach for the remote control.

On the fulcrum there is a hushed timelessness - we are just human – the species embodied in ourselves. In the dawn we'll have re-entered time and consequence. Will jackboots have invaded the Reichstag again? Will we be focused on climate targets, as soil vanishes beneath our feet? Will lovely and ancient carols (dancing songs) be silenced by techno-beat?

Have we decided on the extinction of our own species? That choice is not collective, it is personal.

How will I face my market customers tomorrow, sixty, or seventy percent of whom may have voted jackboots into the Reichstag again, along with a license for the extinction of most of the species of the Holocene – including our own? Will a steely politeness be appropriate – or a wry smile? Shall I say, Have a happy Christmas? For the sedge is withered from the lake and no birds sing.

Poverty will walk into our communities like a deepening frost – life-blood syphoned into the laughing jaws of off-shore hyenas. My Guardian-reading friends will also delight in the spoils, for they helped to create them. Yet, as in 1930, this is democracy. It may be dangerous to speak. The culture will be preserved in tightly-folded papers of samizdat. For the sedge is withered from the lake and no birds sing.

Is this extreme? Yes. It is appropriate. Is this despair? No. It is truth. Only by truth can we hope and hope remains appropriate.

****

Of course, as in 1930's Germany, most who voted for jack boots, had no idea what they'd done – just as the merry laughs which jet to holiday destinations also have no idea what they do. Today, it is worse - in 1930, the vote produced a nightmare - a temporary end of times. Today, the UK vote is for the permanent end of times – full stop – and an end to sweetest dreaming, or nightmares. No generations can fight back, when the previous generation has voted in and endorsed the end of all generations.

However, now we know what we should have known, which is that it is too late for a political process – too late for the IPCC. The coup in the Conservative Party and so also in Westminster has not just happened – it began fifty years ago, in our newspapers, radios and televisions – the generals becoming more and more confident as the years passed. After centuries of utter control, they'd been shocked by democracy into retreat in 1945. Now that democracy is fading, we need a mass exodus guided by common, ancient and filial ethics – a moral movement to leave the Guardian, the Sun, the Telegraph, The Times, The Express, The BBC... unheard and unread. We must build a society, which fits happily within much shrunken demands. Such a thing cannot, and never has happened (successfully) by coercion, advice, imposed tyranny, or the ballot. It is too complex a happening for any but the mingling of personal loves, skills, responsibilities and needs with those of others. Of course, Jeremy Corbyn dreamed just such a movement, which is why the verbal jack boots have spent such energy kicking down the doors of his dream. I am proud to say that I stood by Jeremy Corbyn and have had no time for the yobs and mercenaries of the Guardian and so on, who have destroyed their reputations forever by their efforts to destroy him. In a few decades (how many are left?) they'll attempt to rewrite their biographies. Rising seas may then have engulfed their holiday homes...

So yesterday, before the 2019 election and today, are no different. Our aims are the same and although a more beneficent government may have removed some obstacles from our paths, even so, the currently malignant government will probably not interfere with our choices in how and what we trade, barter and share with each other - that is - how we abandon the enclosures and re-settle the common. In fact, the EU would have been viciously opposed to such an exodus. We can count that blessing.

That, I leave to the next chapter – Reclaiming Capital.

****

CHAPTER 18 – RECLAIMING CAPITAL

It may come as a surprise to most, that my answer for the times is capitalism. What is capitalism? – it is the ethics of a society, whose aim is to maintain its capital – that is, spiritual, pleasurable and human assets, combined with that which maintains all those things – the undiminished vigour of life – in soil, sea, biomass and biodiversity. It may come as an even greater surprise that Adam Smith's capitalism is precisely described above.

You say, how did it go so wrong? Well as G K Chesterton replied to G B Shaw's assertion that "Christianity had been tried and found too difficult." – "On the contrary, Christianity has been found too difficult and has never yet been tried." So it is, with capitalism. No one has tried it yet.

Adam Smith told us that the invisible hand, which moved to the comparative advantages of knowledgeable and settled communities, could not function if...

1. Money ceased to be a medium of exchange and instead became personal property, which could charge rent (interest). "Goods can serve many purposes besides purchasing money, but money can serve no purpose besides purchasing goods."

    Similarly, rent for land, status and ideas, malignantly bleeds beneficent capital of labour, resource and the land. As a later writer pointed out, "Property is theft".

2. If moral probity, ancestral commons and the skill, dexterity and ingenuity of communities rooted in particular terrains, became undermined, or overwhelmed by empire, tyranny of kings, or (as above) by the libertarian power of money.

3. If either dominant leaders, or the more quietly subversive, began to extract – not a just wage, but personal profits.

Adam proposed that the greatest wealth of nations accumulated in societies with low profits and high wages and the least by societies with high profits and low wages.

4.   If (to neatly return to G K Chesterton) monopolies stifled the particular ingenuities and loves of particular terrains.

Here is G K C – *"Communism is Big Business run by the state, whereas, capitalism is the state run by big business. I dream of very many, very small businesses."* Of course, G K C describes the capitalist imposter and not the capitalism *"which has been found too difficult and has never been tried."* Adam's capital moves by the almost infinite complexity of his invisible hand, passing assets between and within the equally complex needs and loves of communities and their terrains.

I make no apology for regularly repeating the above quotes, in this and other passages, because I prefer to excavate my own (limited) memory, which is attached to my more certain and slowly-evolved ethics, rather than seeking the dignity of a false scholarship to shore-up doubtless fragilities. By far the greatest source of knowledge comes by personal perception of people, things and the land, which is then given meaning, for the greater part by simple, inherited family values, which then evolve further as we experience work, joy, grief, love, loss, the wind, sunshine and rain. Books and studies are a pleasure and occasionally a revelation of new possibilities, but always, they are measured against our senses – the actuality of being.

Where we moderns perhaps differ from Adam is in the manufacture of pins – economies of scale – division of labour. We cannot dispute that he is right, but are uneasy. However, if we followed the true logic, then we'd become easier – such efficiencies mean we need less labour and gain increased leisure. History has shown the opposite – increased toil for those who labour, because increased output has not become increased leisure, or increased wages, but on the contrary - increased profit. Pins can also be sold at a lower price, which is to the comparative disadvantage of other, more egalitarian manufacturers of pins. What today, would be regarded as marketing success, would be a cultural failure to the eyes of Adam Smith – increasing both poverty and working hours and also the wealth of one man – the factory owner. Eventually of course, the factory owner would face bankruptcy as his rivals achieved a still lower price. The wealth of all nations, which manufacture pins, would shrink, unemployment would increase, unhappiness would increase.

Ha! - we've seen what Adam thinks of profit, I think he might have said, *Profit is theft* – so yes, he still has the last laugh in the matter of pins and pin heads. And I think, his head is in his hands at our brutish* understanding of the comparative advantages of communities moved (in both senses) by the almost infinitely-complex, invisible, even spiritual hand of moral probity, sacred springs and the musical rhythms of time.

* *I apologise to the brutes of the woods and fields .*

****

Proponents of modelled doughnut, circular and steady-state economies, would do better to bring their models under the beautiful gaze of Adam Smith. All those models fail to confront the certainty that if they became reality, then the collapse of currencies and of currency trading, stocks bonds and shares would follow. With those comes the collapse of real businesses, mass unemployment, crashing tax revenues and of so of vital social infrastructures. So, instead of proposing changes to the current system, we need a movement to evacuate it - to ignore it – to start afresh from the soil upwards as the casino eventually crashes around us.

Of course, capitalism is also a model, but unlike those above, it can only function by that mysterious, egalitarian hand whose energies arrive from many millions of sources, which are all embedded deep in both the culture and its terrain. In current phraseology, it is bottom up, not top down. Because it is an essentially moral system, it needs protection from amorality. That protection can come from both social taboos and from law. So, all we ask of governance is that it is protectionist. As we've seen, durable societies must be protected from profit-making, currency manipulation, share and bond trading, money-property and all other forms of enclosure/monopoly/rent.

Adam's capitalism is essentially moral – in the duties and pleasures of learning/evolving skills to maintain otherwise forever-escaping

78

capital. Capitalism is protectionist. It is conservative. It protects cultural commons from monetarist, corporate/consumerist trade-blocks, such as the European Economic Union. It refuses the free flow of money and accepts the free flow of people and ideas. It refuses property, rent and amoral, immoral casinos and liberates both ancestral commons and the receptive sensuality of commoners to ingeniously adapt to changing times.

We capitalists (Adam Smith and I) use GDP as a useful measure of diminishing capital, increasing CO_2 emissions, shrinking human happiness and increasing money-flow. Increasing GDP means that our economy has been invaded. It means that we must discover where it has been invaded and why. It probably means that money has served some purpose, or other, besides purchasing goods.

As an arrow to true-cost accountants and to those measuring eco-system services, stop it! - that which you'd measure has no price – it is beyond intelligence to measure – it is priceless. Professed measurement diminishes it from the imagination into mere idle fancy. (Please read John Keats and Samuel Taylor Coleridge). All we capitalists know, is that we exist by the beneficence of always mysterious nature and that the source of our existence must be protected at all costs. Natural damage is taboo. Both taboo and ancestral guidance are essential parts of capitalism. Tax-generated cultural commons such as roads, harbours bridges, hospitals, libraries, electricity grids... and so on, are easier to quantify. Commoners have their stake. That stake is human ingenuity, dexterity and labour. It cannot be sold. It cannot add to an expanding GDP. We maintain such capital.

****

CHAPTER 19 – MY WORTHIES, WHAT IS VALUE?

The words, value and worth are used interchangeably and also for both deep and shallow – for that which we love at all costs and also for the relative masses of goods and money.

What is the worth of what I've done? What is the value of what I do? Am I worthy? I don't worry about which word to use and in which context. I think they have survived on my tongue from differing ancestral roots - the one from Old English and the other, Old French perhaps. Both are in use in Middle English. Gwerth is Welsh – old and new.

When we consider the potency of money, perhaps the shallower usage is not so shallow after all. Richard Douthwaite illuminated that money-flow and energy-flow should be directly related. Energy-flow is the power of what people do. Recently, money-flow has vastly expanded, because the power of what people can do has been magnified by fossil-fuelled tools. Plainly, money-flow must rapidly shrink again to just the small power of mortal, fallible humanity. It must fit what the human frame can do to transform only that which can be monetarily valued. Much human activity is culturally valuable, but yet has no monetary value – parenthood, home-making, singing, dancing, walking to the hill-top... So, money flow must be much smaller than even the power of what people do. Such a small flow of money, is very easily managed as a tool to a more complex exchange of labour and resource both within and between cultures. Any community can create its own currency. Within Adam Smith's definition -Goods can serve many purposes, besides purchasing money, but money can serve no purpose, besides purchasing goods. – the creation of moneyed hierarchies is severely limited. Of course, other hierarchies can evolve – military, sexual, religious, and of skills. Some, within a cultural tradition may be beneficial, others not. For instance, we may consider the positions of master and apprentice to be beneficial. How else can an apprentice begin to master her tools?

Meanwhile, that money which now has a purpose besides purchasing goods, must also be out-lawed. It is theft – pillage. What is the power/mass of that money? I don't care. All I know is that it is vast and that we must repel it – it contains money-interest, land rent and rent for the monopolistic enclosures of architects, "consultants", lawyers, medical practitioners... Then we have the money extracted from the casino of stocks, bonds, shares and fluctuating currencies. Shares are an ancient way of launching an adventure – merchant shipping for example. But the buying and selling of shares as chips in a casino is something new – perhaps two hundred years old – its destructive power is plain.

My worthies! We can find a worth, which is beyond price and we can defend it. It is plain that what peer/career-reviewed economics professors call an economy is bound to collapse sometime soon. It has no ground beneath its vast monetary illusion. It is a spun tale, which depends on the complete belief of listening punters. Even so, the collapse will be horrible. It will not be the collapse of a mere illusion, so that truth can finally dawn to contrite visionaries of a new age. Real economic infrastructures will also crumble, causing terrible physical pain. The barbed wires of flailing enclosure will rip open the real economic common. Wages, which once provisioned households to pay taxes, to spend on vital infrastructures, will be gone – leaving fear, anger, confusion, hunger.

That is our task – to build a worthy economy, which fits, just so, inside its ration of Earth. We'll maintain the capital, which we inherited, so that we can bequeath it in turn. There is nothing we can do about collapsing casinos and monetary systems. We must let them fall, while inviting refugees to join us in a new adventure, whose central value is the worth of people and whose central taboo is diminishment of the invaluable – that is the greater ecology on which all species depend.

After the casino collapse, we'll have collapsed systems of distribution. We'll have human misery. But a passing satellite will photograph no change. Roads, streets, houses, bridges, harbours, fields, woods, rivers... will all be unchanged.

We can occupy those commons, each to her skill and with a common vision of the values we had always held, though forgotten in a wild century or two of delusion. In the household we had always understood the fair distribution of chores and pleasures; things and the rationing of things. That is the true economy. We shall make it universal.

Dream on, you say, lost in your dream. Your dream is for the end of times, but with full dignity of office.

****

CHAPTER 20 – ONLY SLOW TIME CAN ANSWER RAPID DECLINE

In every century, historians have mis-told their stories. Their narrative has been of the ephemeral - of what this leader, or that "great general" did to change the course of history. Such tales are useful to leaders. They can be presented at court, admired by politicians and entered as texts in school and university curriculums. They are mirrors for the aspiring to pose their best sides and even, by rote learning of passages – to parade an erudition for the admiration of less "extraordinary" people.

In the same way, narratives are often mis-told by people wishing to change contemporary events – political journalists and theorists, social commentators, "climate change activists" and so on. Those narratives propose that ephemeral action can create durable change. They use the mis-telling of historical events as a precedent to similarly mis-tell the durable changes created by their own political actions.

My readers will know of Fernand Braudel's method for a truer telling of history – of the longue durée - of the deep and slow morphologies of societies above which, short-term and medium-term events and their effects survive for their short and medium terms – having little influence on enduring commons of social behaviour. Tolstoy tells a similar tale in War and Peace. Napoleon can disrupt events by posing as Everyman to vast numbers of followers, but he is nothing to the longue durée. Recent UK & US elections have shown the power of that Everyman stance. The pain (leaving aside climatic tipping points) will come and go.

In his book, Home, Francis Pryor unravels British history in Braudel's way – He asks, what is common to all historical periods? – the idea of home. That simple thought unlocks the past, not as an exotic, but a familiar place – literally - where ancestors like us, in every important way, lived and loved. We find truth in the ordinary – not in praise poems of court bards. We live firstly in families, and only expediently under hierarchies.

In her copious writings of the Fens, – of ancient field systems and commons – Susan Oosthuizen finds archaeological evidence for unchanged settlement, in spite of the spun tales of migration, or invasion – of "Neolithic star gazers", warrior-culture "beaker people", or Saxon "barbarians". These "events" never happened outside history books. She presents archaeological evidence for unchanged field systems, commons and settlements from at least the late Bronze Age until the Early Medieval Period. In her book, The Emergence of the English, she shows how English speaking emerged from the social necessities and fashions of a necessarily tri-lingual people – from Latin, Brittonic and Old English – and that all three languages were probably spoken without effort, even before the Roman (indisputable) invasion of the island. Now, DNA evidence finds no differences between the people of Wales and England – even though Brittonic language survived in Wales and not in England. Language is a useful tool. It does not define ethnicity. It seems the Celtic invasion "event" – bringing Brittonic/Brythonic languages, never happened. Probably, since the Mesolithic, Welsh and English people have stuck fast in their *longue durée* – adopting technologies, gods and languages as time passed. We've no means to know how we spoke then, but we can be almost certain how we thought of home, proper and improper behaviour and the necessity to maintain those commons – common to us and common to them – common to the slow movement of time. I would append that we would have welcomed travellers, traders and traveller's tales. We still do.

Wait a minute! You say, climate change and species extinction need immediate action. We've not time to consider grand notions of deep time. We must sign petitions, appeal to powerful politicians - ask them to "act on the science", because all is now short span.

I say, it is foolish to appeal to Napoleon. We must turn from the ephemeral, to stir the deep time, which flows through all of us. It is foolish to ask leaders to impose a circular, steady state, or doughnut economy, when these things can only be, if we, personally and one by one, live them. The *longue durée* is me and all of us. It is the invisible hand. It is inherited skills - the idea of home and homesmaking, the sanctity of the ordinary, of passing on the ordinary... Leaders can only pervert those things. They have led us astray, so that we created BP, Amazon, Tesco, Renault, Microsoft... by our collective purchasing powers. Leaders cannot create BP and co. Only we can do so and only we can undo so.

The *longue durée* must un-weave the delusive curtains - the sometimes beautifully-woven charisma of Hector, Achilles, Alfred and Arthur; of captains of industry; of Tech Everyman in jeans and trainers. Where a human tool meets its materials is both a sensuality and an ancestry, which joins the species to its soil. It is consequence. We are all consequence. And here's another thing – cultures are what people do to make them. They stop, when people stop culturing. Until the industrial revolution, leaders have not interfered with the making of cultures – that is, with the skills of the trades. Leaders have relied on the autonomy of trades' people without question. They've only distorted it by rent and taxes – and by recruitment to war. But when long-evolved tools, were replaced by new, coal-driven tools, leaders without skills made clumsy attempts at culturing. Now, we have the consequence.

Here, in the *longue durée* what then do we propose? – we people, who G K Chesterton said, have not spoken yet? Do we propose to the powers that they impose a steady-state economy? – knowing that such an action would precipitate immediate collapse of institutions, currencies, stock markets and related companies and the tax-generating wages of those they employ? We also know that the powers belong in the short span - by the mirror of last night's opinion. There is no possibility at all, of their acting on our request.

Instead, we can appeal to each other to abandon suicide and re-learn what drives all durable settlements – commons of good behaviour. It is a moral appeal and could be a religious appeal. Only that central and binding moral can emerge intact as consumerist and monetarist infrastructures collapse tragically around us. They must collapse.

Our time is as epic as those remembered from the flood and the fall, which seem universal to almost all cultures. Science will not help us, nor institutional, or NGO guidance. It is simple – we must quench our fires and re-grow, or let re-grow the biomass and biodiversity of our lovely, singular Earth. The ancestral power of the *longue durée*

85

is in us all. Today, it survives only in the household: in parental guidance, in the rationing of chores and pleasures and in inherited taboos. The household produces children – fully formed into the wider culture. But, as we've seen, a perverted household created Microsoft and Amazon by the power of its spending. Many millions of households did it. Then, schools and universities taught and consolidated the perversion. Education is our flood. Now is the Great Sanity. Un-spend Amazon. Many millions can do it. Where a tool meets its materials comes a spark of truth in educated darkness. First pick up the tools. De-school. Follow the sparks. As the young Geoffrey Hill sang – *"Arthur, Elaine, Mordred, they are gone, under the raftered galleries of bone - and over their cities stands the pinnacled corn."*

Is that extreme? – Well yes. We are at the extreme edge of extinction. That which *"goes on though dynasties pass"* – the pinnacle corn, children laughing at their games, the heaps of couch grass – will also enter oblivion. Leaders will not save them. Only I can. Only you can.

****

CHAPTER 21 – THE WEALTH OF NATIONS COULD BE AN ANARCHIST MANIFESTO

To return to Adam Smith and our chapter – Reclaiming Capital. How would we define Adam's political philosophy? I'd say, it is emphatically anarchist – with expedient compromise. He does not define the wealth of nations. He says, it is in the hands of the invisible hand of cultures settled skilfully and happily in their terrains. He defines only what will prevent its fruition – that is profit, rent, usury, monopoly and an extractive casino of currency fluctuation, stocks, bonds and shares. He says these things must be controlled both by law and the ethics and taboos of cultural tradition.

Pure anarchism hopes for the potency of a common ethic to repel amoral insurgency. Adam is more pragmatic in defining obstacles.

Just as we instinctively know that theft and murder are wrong and so are happy that they be recognised as unlawful, so I think, we also know that usury, monopoly, personal profit and so on are wrong – and that it is wrong that they are not recognised as unlawful. These are ancient cultural taboos. We do not allow them in the household, or in the society of friends. There, ancient commons of good behaviour remain.

In The Wealth of Nations, Adam argues that these things should be criminalised, because they extract money for the benefit of anti-social individuals and to the detriment of society as a whole. They weaken and often destroy the invisible hand and they bleed and sometimes suck dry, the wealth and happiness of nations.

I think his vision is simply true. It is a lesson for our times. Just as in Adam's time, if we asked the powers to introduce laws to criminalise the principle sources of their accumulated and accumulating wealth, we'd be laughed out of the room – or worse. The lesson of the Wealth of Nations was laughed out of the room at the time of publication and in every time since. We've seen the worse in the recent treatment of Jeremy Corbyn, who attempted to introduce a few very mild Adamish restraints to the powers. We'll see the same for Bernie Sanders. In many parts of the world, people presenting such moral reforms are simply disappeared.

But here's a thing – the more people understand the lack of basic moral probity, practiced by business people, politicians and nearly all journalists, so the more, ordinary, moral people will dream of something better. Today's leaders are out-laws in the imaginations of nearly everyone. We know that there is one law for them and another for us. Plainly, removing "them" by violence is certain to bloodily fail. Mass demonstrations may lead to distribution of brightly packaged crumbs, or cheaply manufactured beads– but no more. As we saw in the turmoil of revolutionary Russia, people become forced to take sides. Good people could not but support "communist" factions, because the alternatives seemed far, far worse. Their least-worst option turned out not as they'd hoped, or as the communist manifesto intended. Similarly, but without violence, the Brexit choices were between rocks and hard places - a corporate-supplied, monetarist, consumerist EEU, or an exit to a more extreme version of the same, but led by bankers and stock manipulators, who yet stood as Everymen against "bonkers" EEU legislation. Voters preferred that "human" touch. Humanity is not what they got.

So, Adam Smith's vision of society is utterly true, but is also no immediate help, since violence is the only method by which it could succeed – and so, of course, instantly fail. It remains an excellent guide to good behaviour.

Tipping points for climatic balance and for the survival of very many species, which are part of that balance, have already passed. Permafrost was modelled to melt over half a century in the future. It is melting today. Societies must act instantly to live inside their ecological means. That means radical upheaval for every "developed" economy. Gentle transition is now too late. It means choosing tragic economic collapse and for a Phoenix of our choosing to rise from the ashes (Fire is not the best metaphor and we may not have power to choose). No government will choose collapse. Neither will it choose the end of aviation, the family car, suburbia...

But I can and you can, taking with us the salutary lessons, which Adam Smith outlined as well as anyone in our own times. I hope everyone with deeply-held values will join us. I think that means almost everyone. We hold all the skills. Stock-brokers hold none. We shall de-spend our old lives – in which we spent a corporate invasion into existence. We did that and as I've said, we can undo it. There remains one banner, which can fly into the future – anarchy – the moral fabric of the long durée.

We can live in communities where "work and pleasure are walking distances from everyone's door". We can re-centre suburbia. We can farm and garden properly. We can live within our means. We can become ordinary again. No government can do those things for us.

****

CHAPTER 22 – THE INVISIBLE HAND

Ah, you want me to define the invisible hand? I cannot. It has a depth beyond words and a complexity beyond my singular intelligence. It is the collective hand of all the hands, which create, or diminish the common good. How do we know what is right, or wrong? I can attempt to define how I'd like to steer my own course – and where I've failed, or succeeded. We learn rules of thumb. But some things are deeply wrong, or deeply right. Others are arguably wrong, or right. We discuss them, but can we explain the depth? Those depths, for want of a better word, are felt, not thought. I can live them, but they are beyond the reach of thought. Why is murder wrong? We cannot say. We know only that it is taboo. Some words are evocative, so that a writer can conjure those depths – we re-live them in the best verse, or prose – but still they are undefined. Music does the same.

Without that deep, indefinable truth, societies would fall apart. I suspect that flocks, packs and herds of other species are united by similar convictions. We are all fierce in their defence. For me, the invisible hand weaves the culture from every contributory influence – from all the trades and pleasures, which are guided by a moral common. It is what people do for right, or wrong – its muscular power swelling, or shrinking accordingly. Of course, wrong is often not intended, but is the outcome of a mistake. Mistakes live happily on the common. Do fossil-fuelled tools empower the hand? They do not. They kill it. They have emerged inside the enclosures. Enclosure defines right to irresponsible property. Fossil fuels have not received the moral scrutiny – and the pragmatic trial and error of the common.

How about some similes for the invisible hand? The Holy Ghost: Philip Pullman's dust, or his secret commonwealth; – the workings of the *longue durée*; the bonds of love and family? And then we have a cascade of related words – honour, duty, sanctity, trust, betrayal.

The invisible hand can only live on the common. It is killed by enclosure – starved of contribution.

What about those arguably right, or wrong behaviours? Justification can walk, step by step across enclosures fences into the deeply wrong. We shout - By all that's holy, stop! But justification says, why? If we kill subversives, then peace for all will return. If we charge £290 rent for our status, above our wage of £10 per hour, then we, the wise – the architects, GPs, solicitors and so on, can grow time to think and study. – But I have to work 30 hours to pay for one hour of your time and have no time to study. Precisely, says the solicitor – whose "expertise" is unnecessary to us, but is statutory – statutory to the enclosure. It is crazy and plain wrong to the moral common. It kills the invisible hand.

Simply by that monopolistic enclosure – simply by that new middle class, ancient bonds of society fall apart.

In UK, across Europe and in the US, we've recently seen how that new middle class has taken over the political parties of the Left. It regards itself as educated; as enlightened and forgets to include that it is also rich, by extracting huge rents for its "services". Where can working people go? They belong, they are told by Enlightenment's newspapers, such as the Guardian – to the populist mob.

Here, surrounded by fellow mobsters, John Ball, Gerrard Winstanley, Martin Luther King, we appeal across the fences – by all that's holy think about what you do! But we speak from the heart, from the ancestors, from the secret commonwealth and loved ones at home – without reason; without peer review.

****

VARIATIONS of our THEME

DIFFERING VIEWS – MOSTLY COMIC

FROM

COMEDY, TRAGEDY,

HOME, TRAVEL, COMMONS, MONEY,

COMMUNITY, POLITY, TIME, NATURE, CLIMATE,

FROM THE HABITATION OF HIGH-RISE,

COUNCIL ESTATE AND COTTAGE

AND FROM THOSE WHO RESIDE IN THE
ENCLOSURES.

·A·GARLAND·FOR·MAY·DAY·1895·
· DEDICATED·TO·THE·WORKERS·BY·WALTER·CRANE· ·

CHAPTER 23 – A DAMP LEAFLET FOR A LOST NOTICEBOARD

Trying to change currently enclosed power structures, political processes and systems of information is futile. If we engage with these things, we give them credence. We accept enclosure.

Instead, let's evacuate and settle together on the common. Such a movement exists – apparent in a great diversity of skilled trade's peoples' green and egalitarian feeling and thinking.

It is late – very late, and so every road we take will be through differing forms of tragedy. It is too late for painless transition. Our choice must be the best tragedy – where societies can remain a part of the ecologies, which sustain them.

All our effects must shrink, which means that monetary systems and the casino of stocks, bonds and shares will cascade around us – bringing real tragedy. That is the tragedy we must embrace. All others are far, far worse.

Don't forget, we step into darkness towards a light on the other side. We walk towards delight. We'll not find delight without a passage through the dark. New Year's Day 2020 is dark. Embrace it. We made it. It is ours. Past ways of life made 2020. Now we must end them. Present action creates the future. Action in the dark creates the light.

Until now, we have asked others to create a future for us. We have asked, Tesco, Amazon, BP, British Airways, Nissan and all the rest to make our future. We have paid them to do so. We have commanded them to do so. Without our spending and without our working hours they could not exist. Jeff Bezos did not create Amazon – we did. We are the great mind, or if you like, the complex invisible hand behind it all – the expanding GDP, the crashing ecologies, the extreme poverty, the extreme wealth.

We are the great, subconscious, comfortable, egalitarian master mind of it all.

Wake up. Be conscious.

We have ordered soil to vanish beneath plants and animals, so that soon, we cannot be fed. We have demanded cheap labour manufacturing from opposite hemispheres so that our own skills have died, so that invisible poverty deepens and so that atmospheric CO.2 thickens in a life-stifling blanket.

We have asked that unnecessary life be extinguished by pesticides, fungicides, herbicides and fire, so that social pleasures can thrive – foods and sports and so that eventually, all food, and all sport will be extinguished.

As our own skills have died, we have demanded that our servants, Amazon and etc., use their own skills better to please us. We forget that Amazon ad etc, have no skills, but those we provide. We refuse, preferring dependency – but we depend on empty air.

We subscribe NGOs into existence, as our governmental lobbyists. We rely on their expertise. We sign their petitions. But NGOs have no expertise. Governments have no expertise. Where is expertise? We abandoned it.

We march with Extinction Rebellion, demanding that governments and corporations change to please us, forgetting that it is we who must change. We made the corporation. We spent it into existence. Only we can un-spend it. Extinction Rebellion is a consumerist movement. We must abandon consumerism.

Ah! – but the School Strike is different. Children ask that their parents change. By all that's holy, listen to them!

Lead the children with sheltering arms into the darkness of collapsing infrastructures. Find skills and tools to build human-sized settlements inside humanity's ration of Earth. Let the birds sing. Gather at the piano, to sing our allotted parts of the larger song.

****

CHAPTER 24 – BRIEF INTERLUDE

Yes, "By all that's holy, think about what you do!" we cry as the ageing gas of past fires thickens with the new - smothering the living mass beneath. Once, a vast complexity of species inhaled and exhaled, creating a singular being – a terrain and its atmosphere.

Only connect. We must instantly end the burning, so that the singular being, of which humanity is but one small part, can continue to live and breathe. All the offered dispensations – sequestration, regeneration and so forth, are futile, unless first, we end the burning.

Once we have put out the fires of both life and fossilised life, then we can look around to discover how best to live inside what remains of living cycles and within dramatically shrunken energy supplies. We'll learn from our terrains, how best to eat and excrete, live and die, sing and let sing and by our rations of soil and settlement, to make appropriate tribute in return.

First, we have a great upheaval – all that the fires have given us must end – the family car, aviation, massive shipping, suburbia, commuter culture, the super market, internet shopping, profligate manufacturing, super-human weapons of war. All those things need energy and materials beyond the capacity of a regenerating Earth.

Claims for the virtue, or vice of various farming systems; of people's diets; of techniques for "sequestration" and "regeneration", are all futile if they distract from the urgency of what we face. That is, abandonment of the ways we live today and rapid adoption of ways, in which both work and pleasure are walking distances from everyone's door. Having removed the need for personal transport, we can more easily find ways to live within our means. In countries such as the UK, personal transport is by far the largest consumer of energy. In many parts of the world, it is the least. Only a hundred years ago, in the UK, it was also the least. For most, it was zero.

Then, manufacturing outstripped everything. Manufacturing is created by household demand. There, we have two simple lessons. Most say, it's an impossible and inappropriate lesson. If they are right, then they must accept the mass extinction of nearly all the species, among which, our own has evolved. That includes our own extinction. This is not far off. It has already begun. I think that even seventy-year olds, such as myself, will live to see great tragedies unfold. It is too late for a planned transition. Every year, since the 1992 Rio Earth Summit, CO_2 emissions have risen – dipping slightly in recession – shadowing the expansions of GDPs and GWP. Today, they are over 60% higher than in 1992. Very soon, they will double. Anyone who looks to governments and corporations to find solutions, is plainly crazy. The household holds all the cards.

By household, I suppose a place morally sequestered from the larger goings on of the societies to which they belong. Many of those goings on would be morally unacceptable within the family, (or also friendship groups). In the household we don't charge interest, neither do we accept riches for some members and poverty for others (profit). Instead we fairly ration both what we can have (food, toys, things in general) and what we can do (chores and pleasures) – according to capability.

The ideal village, parish, nation state must surely be a macrocosm of the household. What if, on closing front doors, or garden gates behind us, we carried those deeply understood ethics into the wider world? Poets and philosophers in every time and culture have argued that case. Of course, such movements have been perennially stamped on by the powers. They've also been misused – to supress uppity citizens by political mis-telling of "family values", and so that moral disorder can be "stamped out". But our times are unique – there are billions of households – of course reflecting, in some ways, the cultures in which they are placed, but also (and almost universally) repelling aspects of it – as I've said, of usury, profit and so on. Our times are unique and so what if a unique response is also possible? Never before has the whole of humanity knowingly faced extinction. The case for fair rationing of what we can have and what we can do is inarguable.

****

CHAPTER 25 – HERE'S WHY I'M SO AT ODDS WITH MOST OF MY GREEN FRIENDS

So long as I'm in the fields – in the orchard – or with the animals, I can be happy. I can also be happy in the company of farming people – even though I deeply disagree with their current farming techniques. There is a common ground – an understanding, which I can rarely find elsewhere.

I find the following very hard to untangle. Why do I feel so alienated from most of my "green" friends? I think it is probably in the vagueness of their conviction – in the borrowed nature of it and in, not their lack of experience – because we all have experience, but in their refusal to absorb that experience and instead, rely on the supposed experiences of others. Those others, will have been selected, not for their truth, but for their affinity. This disentanglement of mine, becomes difficult, because such humility is surely a good thing – a route to an open mind and heart. Yet, my friends express those borrowed thoughts with such a sense of virtue that my anger rises. Anger isn't a good thing, so I feel that I've become, as they may truly say, a "negative personality".

Meanwhile, my own experiences have been, for the most part, of personal failure. My conviction, for over fifty years (born 1949), has been this – to find a way of living, which can abandon fossil fuels and also settle happily as a very small part of the re-balancing of a vivacious Earth!

To begin with, as a young man, I thought that growing sufficient food year after year was the foundation of all cultures – so I set out to see if we could achieve crop yields, similar to our neighbours, but without pesticides, herbicides, fungicides and imported fertilisers. I think we achieved that – sometimes receiving 3 tonnes per acre of cereals – sometimes not – because of weather, or my own mis-timings and misjudgements. Of course, if we subtract input from output (which is a truer measure of yield), we came out very well in the balance sheet. To grow an acre of cereals, we needed a further two acres of regenerative crops in rotation, which cut our overall yield considerably – but then, our neighbours in those days followed a similar rule of thumb and did the same. We all grew on so-called marginal, or grade three land. Our "chemical" neighbours did not wish to degrade their soils. Everyone loved their inheritance. Everyone knew of Oklahoma. Everyone, valued their "farm-yard manure". In fact, before we had our own land, I learnt a lot from those neighbours, from years as a farm labourer. Our histories and loyalties are entwined. Together, we've faced fluctuating weathers and similarly difficult prices.

In those days, just about every tenancy agreement, would have a clause forbidding the sale of hay and straw. Everyone agreed that exported biomass should be limited to that extracted for food. Hay and straw should recycle back to soil via animal feed and bedding. That knowledge is as old as the Neolithic – otherwise we must have slash, burn, grow a bit, then move on. In just the last two, or three decades, as with much else, it has been forgotten. Certainly, "climate science" has not re-learnt it – suggesting, as it does, the burning of whole crops (slash and burn) for energy, while calling the process "carbon neutral". Today, the return to soil of human "wastes" is scarcely discussed. Only thirty years ago, I remember, a regular topic of conversation was, of how to remove pollutants from sewage systems. Because solutions are radical, they have been conveniently forgotten.

Very sadly, I feel no such loyalties for my green friends – for their outrageous claims for the carbon sequestered year after year from their borrowed advocacy for this, or that farming system. They defer to this, or that NGO's "selection" of "peer-reviewed" papers on the subject. That phrase – peer reviewed papers – is thought to be a clincher in all arguments. It clinches nothing for me, because the test for all such papers, is to superimpose them on our own experience – to discover if they fit – if idea and substance merge happily together. Sometimes they may do so and we shout, blimey! – that's a new way to think about things. Often, they may not and we must carefully disentangle why that is so. Sometimes too, we must defer to the experiences of others. Always, the measure is against the directly sensual, "actuality of being" – a clumsy phrase, but I have not wit to find another.

Ah well, but I cannot deny that my green friends are seeking remedies to our currently psychotic ways of life – or that my farming friends are often locked in that same psychosis. Our farming neighbours have come to believe that they are the "cutting edge" of the "industry". They've no thought of what's in their drums and sacks, only that they are the latest on the market. As for those pesticides, herbicides, fungicides, growth regulators and artificial fertilisers, they know they are supported by peer-reviewed trials – just as my green friends are supported by other peer-reviewed trials – as the phrase goes, "Peer reviewed trials have shown…". So, the peers are as wildly at sea as the rest of us – at all points of the compass – driven by the winds of career (advancement and wages), fancy, politics… The word, peer, is the clue – no more than gang member of whichever faction we support.

The craziest, cutting-edge fashions practiced by farmers in our region of North Wales are firstly, Maize-growing, for animal feed and also, increasingly for biomass digestors. The necessarily late (frost-free) sowing date means a necessarily late harvest, which as often as not is from water-logged fields. Rivers turn brown and deeply rutted and compacted fields lie bare and puddled through winter. The other, still crazier fashion is for "New Zealand" out-wintering of cattle – fields of Kale down which lines of wrapped silage bales are placed, so that using an electric fence, kale and silage can be foraged together. Fields are usually chosen to be sloping for surface drainage. You can imagine the quagmire of soil and slurry creeping downhill and away. How can farmers do it? I don't know – but it is cutting edge and also peer reviewed.

So I hunch my shoulders and slouch into my dream world, shouting – A plague on all your houses – a plague on those claims for virtuous sequestration from mob-grazed grasslands, because we happen to have some grassland; - from those permaculture plots, which produce so little food, that we'd be better to have a very small veg patch and to turn the rest back into trees; - from the claims of intensive no-dig, heavy-mulch market gardeners, who achieve what they do, by importing vast amounts of biomass from "elsewhere", while not giving a damn about the consequently-impoverished "elsewhere": - from the cutting edge farmers, who've no idea what they do – only that it is cutting edge. *

Trouble is, I cannot put up, or shut up.

Our aim has been to contribute our farm produce towards convivial population centres, where "work and pleasure are both "walking distance form everyone's door" – where workshops, proper shops, market halls and squares are interspersed with libraries, theatres, concert halls, pubs, restaurants, hospitals, meeting houses, churches, temples, mosques... where every street has its corner shop and every village, its workshops, shop, or two, plus pub, church/meeting house... We dream of un-spending the super market and re-spending such places into being, in which every citizen contributes ingenuity and dexterity to the economic whole of both work and pleasure – and in which work herself may become a pleasure too.

And we did partially succeed in our small fragmentary way. We managed to sell all our small farm's produce (just 89 acres), with the exception of cereals, face to face with people over our market stalls. We found many friendships, stories and mutual loyalties through vegetables, apples and apple juice, soft fruit, beef and lamb. Farm and town became, very nearly, in microcosm, one system. We grew and sold, very nearly, a whole cuisine.

But we also failed, because we were compelled to travel further and further afield, in search of busy market squares. Our local towns, though beautiful and ancient places, were also deserted. People congregated in the ringed encampment of barbarian super markets. After years of standing in those deserted and beautiful towns, dreaming of old-fashioned market days, we too betrayed the dream for other, more distant towns, where fragments of dreaming remained. My justification was to promote and participate in the dream, so that as it spread, I could eventually retreat back into my own terrain – just as other producers would occupy my vacated stalls. I maintained that I was on a meandering road to somewhere (home), whereas super markets and internet "organic" box schemes, were locked into a linear road to nowhere.

The dream did not spread. It steadily faded. We were fortunate, because we had gained loyalties and friendships over many years of market trading – and as the towns decayed, so we still maintained fairly steady sales. Newly-arrived producers, in those markets, found it very difficult. Meanwhile, our customers were ageing and one by one, were unable to come to town. Young people (with a few lovely exceptions) did not replace them. Rather, they clicked on the choices of their chosen (usually nation-wide) box schemes, or web sites of artisan producers. We had customers from every class, but without doubt, the greatest volume of sales, were to the so-called working class. That class also paid the biggest personal bills. I suspect that the organic-seeking middle class, followed the young to the internet. They came to us for "another delicious sirloin steak", but it was plain that the bulk of their shopping was done (almost certainly) in the super market. Anyway, the customers with whom we bonded most, were trades' people themselves – who liked to repair things, when broken, who were gardeners and cooks – who had family traditions and loyalties – who were curious about our farming methods – and who were from both the Left and Right of politics. Somewhere in that left and right is a lesson for durable human cultures – and yes, they loved to discuss such things. Our more middle-class customers had more fixed opinions.

Anyway, everywhere I look, the dream is fading, and yet I can see no way to remove fossil-fuels from our culture, other than to remove those ways of life, which need it. The first step must be the footstep (or the cycle peddle). Of course, we can also have oar and sail. We cannot have the family car, commuter culture, suburbia, aviation, massive shipping – and probably, we'll have insufficient energy for the electric railway. We'll discover if that is possible, only after we've found sufficient renewable energy for domestic heat, cookery, refrigeration – and for processes, such as ceramics and metal-working/re-purposing. The first step is to remove the need for personal transport. That is a beautiful first step, because it can be taken personally, but of course, to finally succeed, it will require mass participation – evacuating and re-centring suburbia and re-occupying town and village centres for both pleasure and trade. Market gardens, dairies and orchards can ring those newly-vivacious settlements and we'll also need significant shifts in population towards the countryside as man-power replaces oil-power... Oil-sized farms can beautifully shrink to man-sized (sexless term) and so radical land reforms will be essential.

Populations of many towns and villages are currently too dispersed, but those industrial towns which were built close to sources of coal and iron will have populations, which are far too large for their terrains to supply. Canal and river networks, which were essential to their establishment, may however, assist in the establishment of new, less energy-intensive trades.

This is not a step in the dark. It is a step into what was normal only a handful of generations ago. We know it in our souls. Up until the beginning of the twentieth century – and even in "developed" economies, sail trade remained a significant part of peoples' lives. That's a trade to revive! – and small harbours on every mile of UK coastline await revival for boat/ship-building and for river/canal, shore-hopping and overseas trade.

Don't forget also, that direct traction of water wheels (for instance) may often be more efficient for manufacturing than hydro turbines for electricity to power that manufacturing – Of course such sites can have both – direct power for machinery and small turbine for heat and light.

What a lovely adventure! – which is why my green friends annoy me so much, by their borrowed claims for the carbon sequestered in their virtuous fields. It is not something they know from the trials and errors of husbandry, (the end gauge for everything) but a convenient selection from the literature – from the peer-reviewed trials have shown...

In any case, greenhouse gases emitted from biofuels and fossil fuels so utterly out-weigh even the most outrageous of those claims, that they do no more than fiddle with a more aesthetic arrangement of deck chairs as the Titanic lists further into the icy water.

All agriculture disrupts the natural systems it has replaced. The most a grower can achieve is balance and that is a high and intermittent achievement. My friends say that "science says" they can "draw down carbon" beyond that balance and achieve negative emissions! Well, life can return to lifeless soils – as they say, drawing down carbon, but after a variable period it will end in balance – in optimum biomass and diversity and within the limits of temperature, water and space – simply space (volume of soil). To find and maintain that balance, while also producing food is a noble end, involving many trials and many errors. Often, we may nearly, but not quite, maintain that balance – frequently because of increasingly unpredictable weathers and often, because of our own misjudgements and mistiming.

IPCC relies on those "peer-reviewed papers" and has negative emissions embodied in its modelling. It is no surprise to me that adverse climatic events are arriving many decades before the IPCC prediction. It is not the patient gathering of data, which is wrong – I admire it greatly – it is the entering of that data into models based on untested, yet peer-reviewed/career-reviewed hypotheses, which I have come to despise. Farmers are fortunate, in that the pragmatic tests for life cycle hypotheses, remain on the farm – in the biomass produced season by season in response to their "good or bad" actions. Soil biomass (fungal & etc) and plant/animal/human biomass are one living (and dying) system, with which we attempt, as best we can, to be a part by the best methods of extraction and return. Crop yield indicates both photosynthetic yield and the vivacious mass and energy of the soil life, which produced it.

All farmers know that if we remove a crop for sale and so make no return of biomass to the soil, then next season's crop from that field will be smaller, while next season's photosynthetic power will be reduced and next season's soil biomass will shrink. That is why we need at least two further seasons of regenerative cropping (green manure, or pasture) to return to balance, or near-enough balance. Farmers also know that continuous regenerative cropping (or rather, no cropping) can only end in balance – soil capacity has limits – it will reach saturation, however much solar energy continues to fall on green leaves and however much out-sourced manures, or composts are stolen from neighbouring life-cycles.

IPCC use an untested hypothesis in all their sequestration models – they say (they really do!) that if land-use is unchanged, then we can extract crops year after year and the system – the life-cycle, will remain in balance. They say the same for coppicing, or clear-felling of forests – worse, future models include negative emissions by carbon capture and storage from the burning biomass, such as forests, or biofuel crops.

I can find no IPCC reference to trace where extracted biomass ends, or returns to an agricultural life-cycle. Food crops end in food "waste" and sewage "waste". Burnt biomass ends in energy, gas and ashes. That gas, they say, is balanced by the photosynthetic powers of trans-substantial leaves – an immaculate conception - a holy ghost of CO_2 miraculously regenerating clear-felled, or stubble soil.

As I say, farmers and growers test the IPCC hypothesis, year by year in crop yields. Climate models are wildly optimistic. Why is there no outrage from farmers? I suppose, convenient untruth, is better left sleeping, while we lobby for government subsidy for our "carbon farming".

Anyway, in case some think problems are too immense for the individual to be a part of solutions, here are some UK government statistics, which show the opposite – that only the individual and the household have a hope in hell of solving them. I've lazily lifted these figures from a previous book of mine and so they are a year out of date. I don't think it matters…

Here are DBEIS figures for UK energy consumption (their categories and terms).

Transport consumes	40%
Domestic	29%
Industry	17%
Service	14%

If we break down the transport figures, we have

Domestic	65%
Industry	21%
Service	14%

So, if we break down domestic, industrial and services to include their transport consumption, we have

Domestic	55%
Industry	25.4%
Service	19.6%

So, households directly control more than half of total energy consumption. What's more, households control a very high proportion of all the rest by the power of their spending. Very plainly, personal transport and personal expenditure on manufactured goods and services are controlled, not by governments and corporations, but by ordinary people. Ordinary people are far from powerless. I think we hold nearly all the powers. We can un-spend most of our difficulties – which, like Amazon, Tesco and BP, we had previously spent into existence and we can congregate in more convivial places – re-spending around us, new (sometimes old as the hills) dexterity, ingenuity and artistry. Of course, much economic activity is and always has been, moneyless. That too is exclusive to the loves and needs of community. Government, corporation and bank are excluded from that influence.

The reason why UK performs so well (in published carbon budgets) relative to other nation-states, is that out-sourced manufacturing is not included in the above figures. UK manufacturing has declined dramatically in recent years – far more rapidly than similar European economies. Once, it was the largest UK energy consumer. Now, offshore purchasing is largely in the hands, not of governments and corporations, but in the clicking buttons and key boards of UK citizens and so our powers are even greater than those suggested above.

Yet, we ordinary people lobby governments, politicians and corporations to change, when we, the lobbyists, hold most of cards for that change. I suppose, we've been educated to think otherwise – peer-reviewed papers have shown. No one is de-schooling. Why aren't my green friends de-schooling. As W B Yeats sang, we could say of every trade,

Irish poets, learn your trade. – Sing whatever is well-made. – Scorn the sort now growing up. – All out of shape from toe to top. – Their un-remembering hearts and heads. – Base products of base beds.

That's why I'm so depressed and grouchy.

****

I know that there are many fine, food-producing permaculture practitioners, many excellent do-dig systems and that many others add to overall productivity in their skilled use of grasslands, but none of these can achieve so called, negative emissions. All systems end in balance. Even the wild will end in balance. Our aim should be optimum (durable maximum) life – in both its biomass and energy. To subdue our hubris, we must acknowledge that the greatest vivacity will always be found in the evolved complexity of the wild. Human systems will always disrupt that evolution and the most elegant of human systems can only ever arrive at a balance, which has a lower overall biomass and energy than the natural system it has replaced. People have always known this. Stories of the Fall are universal. Physicists and "bio-chemists", thinking only of carbon have persuaded people otherwise. In the face of thousands of years of agriculture, the physicist is clearly ridiculous.

CHAPTER 26 – THE IMMACULATE CONCEPTION

From now on I shall refer to the immaculate conception by the holy ghost, which is the central pillar (no phallus intended) of climate and carbon sequestration models employed by IPCC, ZCB 2030 & etc, as ICHG.

The Zero Carbon Britain model employed an increase in biofuels. It proposed to introduce bio-fuelled aviation at a third of the then current, total capacity. It rated those biofuels as "zero carbon". In response to my 2010 inquiry to CAT they kindly sent me this –

If biomass is burned, the chemistry is more or less reversed, and the original energy and raw material (CO_2 and water) are released. There is then no net gain, or loss of CO_2, which is why biological fuels are considered to be carbon neutral. That the hypothesis is ridiculous and that it is not even framed as a life cycle, (rather as a carbon cycle) has been the reason I began to write in the first place. I've spoken of it copiously since 2005. I won't bore you with more of the same. Rather, I'd like to consider it as a moral proposition.

My right, or wrong actions on the farm are important to me. Moreover, the farm is a perfect environment to test the ICHG hypothesis. I'll bore you a little more by mentioning that the ICHG hypothesis has never been tested in the peer-reviewed literature. Rather it is a blindly accepted assumption from the scripture. When did it begin and who first proposed it? – I've no idea. An eloquent and loved A level science teacher? Perhaps it was she, who first chalked the script on a blackboard, so that it became a contagious light bulb in the minds of her pupils. To have become universally accepted, I'd guess she flicked the switch, sometime in the 1960s, or 70's.

I think it originates in worship of human ingenuity and the substitution of an equivalent ingenuity in nature – nature as narcissistic mirror – clever photosynthesis – the copious linear gift of sunlight, which forever heals life's broken cycles. Look! – leaves are like solar panels – clever as people, says a father to his child. It is a Cauldron of Ceridwen from which we can feast forever, because it remains, forever full. Perhaps it should also be known as the Ceridwen Hypothesis. It encapsulates Hubris to end all hubris.

I think that a universal moral awakening – a religion – is our last hope for human cultures to shrink their needs to just what a terrain can supply. ICHG is not that religion.

Nemesis knows that if we burn a field, or forest, we will be left with gas, energy and ashes. Nemesis knows that ashes (if we're very lucky) are an insufficient return to our field, and that the whole life-cycle of soil, plant and photosynthetic power will shrink – simply for a lack of life. Next season's biomass in soil and so plant will consequently shrink. Photosynthesis will be limited to just that shrunken unfurling of green leaves. Nemesis also says that this is not a straight line of decline: it is parabolic – it accelerates through tipping points to Oklahoma. The linear gift of sunlight is limited by the cyclic, living mass of green leaves, which receive it. The linear is limited by the cyclic. How much living mass (or humus) is sequestered in the wind-born soils of Oklahoma? Oklahomans followed the ICHG hypothesis. They were forced to starve, or migrate.

Nemesis also knows that the most vivacious life-cycle is limited by soil volume, water and temperature. Once the cup of soil is full of life, it can increase no more. However much we think we add to our soils by importing compost and manures, once soils are in balance at optimum capacity, the cup will run over. Photosynthetic leaf area will not increase. It will import no more sunlight. Worse, that imported biomass will have been stolen from a consequently impoverished soil in another's field. Fair distribution in agriculture is the primary model for personal ethics – for the laws of commons.

Some consequences of belief in Ceridwen's never-empty pot of soil are –

Life can return to degraded soils, by re-wilding, or by better husbandry. In IPCC terms, this is called sequestration. So far, so good. I agree. However, since IPCC also believe in the cauldron, they

110

project that same sequestration into the future – even after a system has attained balance and soil capacity is full. I do not agree.

Neither a rainforest, nor an imagined perfectly-balanced agricultural system will sequester any further carbon. That fictitious "draw-down" cannot be set against fossil fuel, or biofuel emissions. IPCC climate models are consequently wildly optimistic.

Burning fossil and biofuels is simply wrong and no pardons, or indulgencies can mitigate that wrong. Burning fossil fuel is far better than burning biofuel, because, in consequence, living systems can be left to live and breathe. I do not advocate burning fossil fuels.

Claims by many permaculturalists, organic farmers, and grassland polemicists that they can "draw down carbon forever", is wrong. They can do so only to an optimum point of balance and that balance will be a very high achievement. Frequently, adverse weathers and human misjudgements will leave them (and with the best intent), the wrong side of that balance. Those who import fertility in out-sourced composts and manures, impoverish that neighbouring cycle. The exporter's overall biomass will deteriorate faster than the importer's biomass can regenerate. The sum of biomass in both systems will be smaller than before the import/export "event". We accelerate to Oklahoma by unpredictable tipping points in the web of life! Death is quick. Life, though powerful, is slower.

It should be a moral calling – an honour, to guide a farming, growing, or forestry system towards balance. It is no shame to sometimes fall short of that balance. We are fallible – the thing is, to try. However, as many do, to claim negative emissions is deeply wrong. It is outrageous. Some carbon footprint calculators will tell you that virtuous acres of imported biomass (carbon) will provide dispensation for your family car, or a couple of holiday flights. I don't like the word evil, but at last, in that case, the idea is evil. The people who adopt it are very dangerously deluded. I include IPCC, Zero Carbon Britain 2030 and many others in that category.

****

CHAPTER 27 – A BRIEF HISTORY

I suppose that since agricultures began, people have pillaged their soils and stripped landscapes for fuel and building material. Of course, others have warned us to think of tomorrow – the terrain that feeds us, must be fed in return. Everywhere, laws of commons evolved for fair (or at least, agreed) distribution and rationing of water, arable land, grazing, timber and other foraged and mined resources.

It seems that round 1500BC, warrior hierarchies and cults emerged from friction between neighbouring communities. I imagine that communities farmed, manufactured and traded much as before, so that we cannot say "warrior cultures". It is probable that tree-cover then, in what is now the UK, was pretty much what it is today. Land competition began. Since then, forests have grown and shrunk by human activity - or occasionally, the lack of it. By the Seventeenth Century the land reached "peak bleakness" – stripped of trees for fuel, house and ship-building. Economic collapse was inevitable, but then – a miracle - coal reprieved both the economy and to an extent, the forest.

Now, we struggle to unwind that industrial revolution. We find ourselves pretty much back in the Seventeenth Century, with a larger (but still very small) forest, but also with a population about fourteen times larger. Do we have greater knowledge? I don't think so – or not much – most of our new tools, methods and thoughts have been tied to coal, oil and gas. We do have some new electrical tools. The internet? – I doubt we've electrical capacity to power it. We've more urgent new electrical demands – domestic heat and cookery and then, ceramics, smelting... I doubt there'll be any to spare for transport – and if there is, it must be severely rationed in some way.

We've gained new insights into biological systems, but there again, we've also lost many. How do we treat the land? I cannot think we know much more than Galen in the first century AD and Virgil in the first century BC – and they were both very far from "expert". Still, we must farm by rule of thumb, returning a biomass equivalent to the mass we extract. Thinking of biomass – plainly, we cannot burn it, but it can be fermented, and so return digestate to the soil. Domestic gas for cookery is a simple and elegant technology and "farm-yard" gas may be sufficient to power some small machinery.

That burnt fermentation gas would rise anyway – all biomass must ferment, producing humus, minerals for plant growth, heat and gas to the atmosphere... If we gather "waste" biomass, we can substitute gas from aerobic fermentation with gas from our anaerobic fermentation. Then digestate can return to the aerobic cycle again having lost what we have gained – a little gas and energy. In the scheme of things, that is probably a small disruption.

Meanwhile, greenhouse gases from human cultures are rising so fast that we have very little time. We must stop burning both biomass and fossil mass – on an instant (15 years). Zero emissions by 2035, mean just that – not the net zero of IPCC. On reaching optimum balance, an ecosystem will be just that – balanced. It will "draw down" no further "carbon". Neither a perfectly imagined agricultural system, nor a vibrant rain forest will help us. They will be saturated with life – at the limits of soil volume, canopy area and so on.

Of course, we can heal our broken cultural cycles – returning life to degraded soils – and that, it is true, will "draw down carbon". But there again, the harm is something we have done, which we must now undo. It will be hard work. There will be no lazy negative emissions from "Nature's ecosystem services" to save us. This is cultural – or mis-cultural – we can retrace our steps to where and when we misbehaved a lot less and resume from there. Even so, we'll have still more to change. For instance, if we alight in the Seventeenth Century (UK), we must quench those domestic fires – fourteen times as many domestic fires... However, we'll have a culture which can thrive without the family car, aviation, massive shipping, the internet... We'll have sail-trade, mostly manual farming systems, manufactories powered by wind and water, local self-reliance, anciently-evolved trades.

The advantage of imaginatively returning to the past, is that we retain a deeply-understood cultural tradition. So, we'll remain with inefficient hierarchies, enclosure and social injustice! But then, we'll have the same old commons of good behaviour and a yearning for the common good. We'll have hope for change within a durable economic foundation. Today, there is only shame and despair.

****

CHAPTER 28 – LOCK-DOWN - THE FIRST FAINT WHISPER OF HOPE

For zero cultural CO_2 emissions, plainly we must change the culture. I'd say, we must evacuate the culture and occupy another, so that human causes sit inside a ration of Earth. It is futile to think we can electrify what we have. What we have is no longer possible. It never was possible. We've lived a lie – a vicious lie. Few of us want to be vicious. Well, let's evacuate and be what makes us happy – to be kind.

To live within our ration, we must also abandon those parasitic hierarchies, which prey on balanced and circular economic activity – rent for enclosures of money as property (usury), land as property (rent) and status as property (rent for professional status in law, medicine, architecture, planning...) Without that abandonment, we'll not live within our earthly means. We must pillage to pay rent.

Coronavirus has forced some steps towards living within our ration, suspending some of the parasitism listed above. And, we've seen banking and aviation teetering on the brink of collapse. If we are to stay within two degrees of warming, we've only fifteen years to plan their demise. Is that possible? It is not likely – near impossible. Collapse is the miracle we need – the only practical solution. To live a good and kindly life, we must pray for the miracle. Remember, two degrees of warming will still be highly unpleasant. It means the flooding of coastal and island communities – violent storms, terrible droughts.

The tragedy of casino collapse, means that people may come together to build their own economy on solid ground. By casino, I mean usury, currency manipulation, trading of stocks, bonds and shares and the gambling on rising rents. Those rents are extracted from wealth gained by true economic activity. Most powerful politicians, journalists and "business" people today, belong, not in

115

the economy, but in that casino. To be plain, they have no sense of reality, levitated as they are on an upward flow of money from the real economy, which they predate.

In my dream, the ethics of home and family – the fair rationing of land, food, things, chores and pleasures, become the model for a renewed economy – the good housekeeping of every trade and governance. It means the return of the common and the end of enclosure. It is a very strong dream, because I think nearly everyone has dreamed it – as Rob Hopkins says, *what if?* It has recurred throughout history and in every place, but it has been almost universally supressed from reality. Today, if it does not become reality, then two degrees of warming will very swiftly become four and it will be sans dreams, sans history, sans future, sans everything. Remember, we've only fifteen years to shrug off the parasitism and to live within our physical means.

Coronavirus illuminates both the possible and the likely. They are far from the same. I'll not hide it. My heart is breaking. Here in the UK, many people are behaving very badly indeed – fighting over what seems, in the end, most precious to them – toilet rolls. Government looks likely to behave very badly indeed by pouring billions into airlines, corporations and banks. Toilet roll manufacturers have done quite well and have asked for no support. It seems everyone needs their suicidal way of life, fearing the virus and its effects, but having a kind of hysterical, psychotic forgetting of the utter terror they will cause, only a few decades away. It is not lack of education. The major causers of climate heating are the climate-educated middle class and the rich. In that category, I include every jet-setting climate activist, and every "climate scientist" who has attended any Earth Summit, since 1990. Plainly, they've not changed a thing. Surely, they must also own large stashes of casino money, to afford both those fights and the leisure to make them. They are rather like those New Labour politicians, who have destroyed the Labour Party with the backing of Mr Rupert Murdoch. The consensus of IPCC is to green the status quo with the backing of "industry".

But many other people in the UK are behaving very well, devising networks of support – that is living a good life by their "family values" – acting out commons of good and kindly behaviour – without support from government, corporation, or bank.

116

What if – instead of massive gifts of money for suicide, authorities put the same (I think much less would do) into the inherited skill, ingenuity, dexterity and moral probity of communities, so that what is parasitic on those things would collapse and something beautiful, true and appropriate could emerge from beneath the ashes?

Coronavirus has forced some governments to do just that – suspending parasitic activity (rent, mortgage and so on) and providing cash for those who must isolate from their work places.

In developed economies, most manufacturing is destructive and useless. Most travel is destructive and useless. Most "economic" activity is destructive and useless. What if – we decided to live good, happy and kindly lives together. It is a very, very powerful and also a very ancient dream and it is, yearningly – just faintly stirring – a possibility. But first, we must actively choose "economic" – that is, total casino collapse – total collapse of the ways we developed and so-called, educated people live today. Viewed from a passing satellite nothing much will have changed. Fields, woods and the solid infrastructures of towns, roads, harbours, bridges... will all remain untouched – awaiting occupation. At night, many pinpricks of light will be quenched and at day those vapour trails, which were once teased out by the wind into semblance of cirrus clouds – will be gone.

****

CHAPTER 29 – CONVIVIAL REVELRY IS NO SMALL THING

Once upon a time, not so long ago, economic transactions using money, were out-weighed by economic transactions, which did not. Still, that moneyless economy, though much shrunken, remains a force for good. Without it, the whole edifice of wages, spending, rents, money interest, stocks, bonds and shares would collapse. Today, because money has accelerated beyond control, "economies" are teetering on the edge of collapse. As we know, parenthood is often deferred to paid child-minders, nurseries and schools. Music is bought in concert tickets and recordings, while singing around the pub piano is a distant memory. Apprenticeships have been replaced by expensive and inappropriate university courses. Monopolies of medicine, law, architecture and so on, charge fabulous rents, merely for their enclosed social status – and of course, much else for which people are paid wages, is futile, ugly and useless.

Only sixty years ago half the population remained at home, without wages, yet working full time - cooking, caring, teaching, washing, cleaning, telling stories, singing nursery rhymes... But for the upper middle class, half the population (women), probably worked harder than wage-earning men. So, in the above respect, unpaid work outweighed the paid. Add to that football, cricket, productive gossip, pub sing-songs – yes, I agree, women often missed out on those things too.

Let's fade back into the Thirteenth Century, when, as David Fleming has eloquently reminded us, a massive part of everyone's time was passed in religious and seasonal festivals. Economies were hugely resilient, because money was but a small part of the whole. Always, when things went wrong the unpaid probity, ingenuity and dexterity of people could step in.

Don't mention medieval hierarchies and the unjust distribution of male to female labour. It's plain - so we can change it for the better. In any case, hierarchies today are spiralling out of control by pillaged and utterly irresponsible wealth. A lord of the manor had function and obligation and was, in any case, poor by today's standards. In medieval times, (I speculate) Richard Branson would be imprisoned (or executed) for transgression of common law. We are not performing well on the male/female balance either...

Truly, I can see no alternative today but to resume such models. Though money is useful for more complex trades in scarcity and surplus, a so-called steady state, or circular economy must be largely moneyless to achieve resilience to the unexpected and also to achieve self-determined happiness. If every household had a garden, some musical instruments, a store of ancestral tales and rhymes, surely that household would also produce new songs, tales and rhymes of its own. The stimulus would not be money, but conviviality.

Of course, if half of us – a mixture of men and women - worked for money, eight, or so hours a day for four, or so days per week, producing, by our various skills, what our communities need in the way of food, fabrics, furniture, metal work... and that money circulated entirely within that exchange of trades - but for a tax – say a tythe, or perhaps more - as contribution to common infrastructures of hospitals, harbours, libraries, irrigation sluices, bridges and so on, money which, in consequence, would cycle back again - then still that activity would be a small part of a twelve-hour seven-day whole, which one half of the adult population would have for pleasure. The other half of the population would have similar pleasure time (slightly less?). But their day jobs of cooking, cleaning, caring would involve no money.

I do think, we need to welcome the return of uncensored long sentences along with long balmy Summer days to sit by the river and practice the fiddle, or to stroll into a deepening intimacy with our landscape, or to read and write and tell each other stories of how these things came to be. You bring the wine. I'll bake the bread.

As the world sits in coronavirus lock-down, a common Guardianist (short) sentence is – "You said the economy was everything, now we can see that it isn't." As usual the Guardian is wrong. The economy is everything, but the greatest part of that economy must be moneyless. The true economic dynamo is common understanding of good behaviour, which needs no payment, and is certainly its own reward. Good behaviour makes the culture. Bad behaviour erodes it. Yet, Left Liberals would put money value on "eco-system services" by their "true-cost accounting". They lobby for basic income for house-keepers. They lobby for more money. It's true that basic income is a temporal remedy to social injustice and it's also true that it can stimulate real economic activity. It's true that it's the best course in our current shut-down. But if that money is created by central banking, it will simply add to the mass and power of money. If it is generated by a tax on enclosure, as Tom Paine tells us, money flow would remain the same, while its restorative justice could add (it also may not) to commons of good behaviour.

The truth is that increasing money flow by adding still more fictitious "natural capital", would be another step over the edge for the soon-to-be crashing casino. Commons of good behaviour teach that the ecology of which it is but one small part, is priceless. Reverence is useful. It has proved effective in just about every culture, every-when and everywhere.

As we've explored, much else is priceless too – parenthood, the delight of attained skill, bonds of friendship and family, the sight of a good crop of corn, laden apple trees, well-brewed beer, a lovely fabric, a dove-tail joint well-fitting, tale-telling, music, dance...

As T S Elliot's friend, Ezra Pound (forget the politics) attests, *"With usura hath no man a house of good stone."*

Money as a tool for more complex exchange than barter, is liberating and useful. Money as property is an always destructive power. Enclosures of money, land and status into irresponsible property are at the chore of our amoral pillage of both nature and each other. Present action creates the future, just as past action created our present.

The reason I slid so easily into organic farming and subsequently became so alienated from most "new" organic farmers, is this, my definition of the word, organic –

Organic – *method, which seeks efficiency and resilience, by imitating the cyclic behaviours of organisms.* Organic as a method applies to everything – to every trade, infrastructure and pleasure. Its primary attitudes are reverence, belonging, study and the learning and application of skills. Such a definition was commonplace to agriculturalists of the 1930s, 40s and 50s. By 1990 it was utterly betrayed. It had entered the market-place and wanted as much of it as it could. How that market was "organised", or rather disorganised, was of no concern. I remember, David Fleming as a solitary voice of discontent at one packed Soil Association meeting. I loved what he said, though what it was escapes my memory. Anyway, it's a comfort to me now that I have his writing. My younger, and shy in public, conviction is affirmed. As Wendell Berry says, Eat and you are involved in agriculture. We might as well add, Eat and you are involved in everyone and everything.

****

CHAPTER 30 – DARING TO DREAM

While coronavirus forces us into isolation, many things may become apparent, which were previously supressed from the imagination.

1. Isolation-enforced de-growth may lead to an imagined and personally-planned de-growth, in which moneyless activities, far outweigh the moneyed. Natural pleasures may become more valued goals – than the old goals of pursuing money to buy manufactured pleasures.

2. The above will become acute (rather than chronically simmering) if our chronically unstable "economies" crash, leaving acute trauma. Moneyless activity may prove both more productive and more felicitous, than violent scrambles for money and limited supplies. Of course, that last may win out, but it is not irrational to dream that it won't. In any case, if the current "economy" does not crash, our planet will very soon be uninhabitable. We must imagine and hope that it will crash. That tragedy is our best hope. We must choose tragedy. It is time to imagine tragedy as benign.

3. Enforced family and community rationing may lead to self-reliance in many other things too and to a mistrust of plainly inept governments and of their advocacy for amoral corporate supply - and also to their class-enforcing doctrines. For instance, in states, such as the UK, revulsion at its corrupt newspapers and radio/television channels, may lead to a new thirst for self-learning and to a delight in it. Similarly, expensive and time-wasting education, which teaches us to conform to the current status quo, may be seen for what it is. On the schooling ladder we must conform to pass exams and later, we will find it advantageous to seek, not peer-review, but career-review.

Something is rotten in the state of UK. Imagine a return to health – to good, honest, timeless decency. Imagine it.

4. The fantasy, which we so vociferously call, the bottom line, progress, enlightenment... may be seen as the fantasy that it is. Currently, we see climate heating as an abstract idea, and the lives, which cause it, as solid reality. For most of us, our lives will outweigh a mere idea.

What if the scales fall from our eyes and we suddenly see, zero emissions (not net zero) by 2035 as an urgent reality, and our lives as dangerous fantasy?

****

CHAPTER 31 – THE WRONG KIND OF PANIC

This is a panic pandemic. Be still everyone. Listen quietly. You are distracted. What's that approaching thunder? It's the heating of the world - flood, famine, unbearable temperatures, then RIP humanity. We can only escape it, if we achieve zero human emissions by 2035.

I don't mean net zero emissions, I mean zero. I mean that you and I must find ways for both work and pleasure to be "walking distance from everyone's door". Nothing less will do. Nature will not save us with a dispensation sequestration – with a pardon, or indulgence from the Offices of Soil. We did what we must now undo. Afterwards, we'll see if we can humbly sit within her laws with a minimum of our old disruptions. We've been utterly unruly.

Today, we drilled spring corn and combining peas – life goes on, even in this panic pandemic, dozens of linear vapour trails crossed an otherwise clear blue sky. Evidently, we have not panicked enough, although the virus has forced us to curb some profligate behaviours. Shut your eyes and listen to that blackbird sing – our next Amazon purchase brings closer, the end to such lovely things.

To be sure, we are self-isolating – leaving produce in the honesty box at the head of our lane – our son has not completed his chemotherapy and his parents are seventy-year olds. But I cannot fathom why 2020's virus is any worse than those of recent years. There's something fishy in the state of Denmark, though what it is, I haven't a clue. Skulduggery is supposed to be silent and invisible to an ordinary geezer, like me. Yet, conspiracy theories pervert true thought.

It's strange for anyone to say, the world will end for humanity – it should be ridiculous. However, it is simple truth.

However, it seems that everyone has a new dispensation for delaying a response – some newly-powerful negative emission hidden up their sleeves, or a convenient virus to "force us" to look the other way.

No state in Erd here stadis sicker
As with the winde, wavis the wicker
So wavis this worldes vanitee
Timor mortis conturbat me

****

CHAPTER 32 – WHO OWNS THE ME OF ME?

How do we trigger a thirst for knowledge and so of particular remedies, particularly-applied to particular problems? Not by education. Education, alongside rent for almost universal enclosures of land, money and "educated" status, have together made such ingenuity the exclusive property of both the educated and the landed/moneyed. Other knowledge is thought to have no "authority". In short, the unique experiences and perceptions – the intelligence of un-patented people is thought to have neither autonomy, nor personal authority. The patent – the licence; the ownership; the doctorate, is everything. Commons of ancestral (not ephemeral) guidance, family and cultural traditions and of the moral probity and skills of the trades have been excluded to the shanty town. It is an apartheid system. All that has not been enclosed is crowded into an amusing and tiny village green. The economy survives there, (comically) as it can – earnestly told to live within its means, while the casino of rising and falling currencies, usuries, bonds, stocks and shares, governs people's lives. It does not "govern the world". It is unaware of the world. It has no intelligence of it. Species cascade, CO_2 is wildly disbalancing, human food sources rapidly decline, poverty accelerates, and all the while no authority reacts. For instance, "climate change scientists" publish interesting papers about climate into a world of enclosed ideas without substance – negative emissions, CCS... All is levitated into the modernist dream. Enlightenment need not touch the ground, where the ordinary people live. The thing about modernity is, it sleeps, out of time, perennially in the past. For about two hundred years it has remained an impossible slumber. Now, it will destroy itself.

Truly, I think that schools and universities are killing solutions to the causes of species extinctions and climate heating – that is, our profligate lives and their effects. As R D Laing said all those flowery years ago, *"The life I am trying to find, is the me, who is trying to find it.*" Similarly, we can say, the solution I am trying to find is the self, which is trying to find it. Who else knows my life, but me? Who else has power to change me? Who but me, can stop me taking that holiday flight? Modernity's enclosures banish the me of me to the shanty-town. Only there, in that pocket-handkerchief of common can I reclaim it. From there we must expand. We must choose the ridiculous, because as G K Chesterton might have said, only in the ridiculous, can we make sense.

That could be the climate activist's slogan – "Who owns the me of me?" Respect for the career-hungry and ridicule for truth-hungry innocence is creating an economy, which is blind to reality and fervent for the received enlightenment of career/peer-reviewed ideas. Of course, innocence is the truly receptive state. It fits the territory, we now inhabit - uncharted by anyone, anywhere, and any-when in history. It truly is Cloud Cuckoo Land – a place where the poor people live. It is the second part of the new two-part class system, to us, it has returned to them and us – to them in those rent-gathering enclosures, it is progress, enlightenment and modernity on the one hand and the mob (populism, dependence, activism) on the other.

Another slogan could be – "Cloud Cuckoo Land is the only land". As often though – only the clown and the child can speak truth to the king. After your first joyous footstep – one that is yours and yours only, will you retreat back into the enclosures, afraid of the ensuing, peer-reviewed and to the human soul, utterly-chilling laughter.

****

CHAPTER 33 – THE CHOICE IS BETWEEN A TRAGIC RITE OF PASSAGE OR EXTINCTION.

A lovely morning to greet Easter Sunday. Yes, I can live in the moment of birdsong & young blossom and for a moment, be happy. But, how many more spring festivals shall we celebrate? My lack of action - my unchanged life will soon (has already caused) the end of all dawn choruses and of all festivals. Pompous? Really?

There is a way "to flatten the curve" on climate heating - forget flattening the curve of the virus - good behaviour for that is now second-nature - & to think about how to personally abandon the family car, how to make flying an historical anomaly & how to make trades & pleasures to be within walking distances. That, not ephemeral virus behaviour, should be our deepest second nature.

While we have leisure of lock down - here's some productive planning. How do we re-centre suburbia into self-sufficient towns & villages and create more horticultural, more dog & stick farming systems, re-populating fields with people, not oil? How do we replace car parks with allotments and market gardens? How much can both domestic and market gardening weave into the town? How do we import food and return manufactured goods to and from surrounding fields and orchards and back, without fossil fuel?

How do we replace the manufacture, or import of useless goods, with both more productive and self-determined labour and also with the resultant leisure time? After all, even today, unpaid labour and self-made pleasures, make up the greatest part of our "economy". Increase that time and we create a more resilient, skilled and convivial economy, which is less dependent on external forces, such as money. David Fleming calls such a way of life, the slack economy. It has leeway. It can stretch and contract without collapse, because the skills and morals of people will have replaced "the market". People are always available to "step in". Someone's senses, everywhere and anywhere will note economic weaknesses and someone with specific skills will find remedies. An economy is an organism connected to its terrain as best it can – it is the causes of one species in constant adaption to its ecological effects. It is fallible. It is a eusocial adaption – not one of the sum of individuals, because sensual intelligence must first pass through the senses of someone. But if that individual is connected. Yes. Only connect.

Casinos of usury, rent, currency manipulation & gambling of stocks, bonds & shares, have bled the real economy of people, their trades and pleasures, dry. Here, in the reality of fields & lost trades, why not, when we can, use money as rebellion? Spend it between ourselves. Create an economy beneath casino collapse. We can un-spend the corporation, the solicitor, the architect and so on – out of existence, and re-spend a convivial community into existence as the ashes of wealth extraction fall around us. Modernity is levitated above and apart from the vital movement of time. It is locked in the past, forever seeking the future of progress, and enlightenment. It is about to destroy both itself and our species.

We can evacuate, descend and stand in the moment amidst her sensual rewards. The moment is the only vital time/place. Only the present moment can make the future, just as our present is groaning with the clumsy missteps of the past. Many of those footprints will have been our own. So, step lightly and the future will not have to bear that weight. Step into the moment of the species and her ecological effects. Tragedy is everywhere. It is the truth. We cannot but choose tragedy – all other roads are blocked – transition is too late – de-growth to a steady state economy is too late. We must choose the collapse of modernity – the collapse of all that weight of money, worthless work, rent, stocks, bonds, shares... It will bring horrible suffering – unemployment, crashing tax revenues and so collapsing infrastructures. But our choice is that suffering, or worse - extinction not only of our species, but nearly all the species with which, together we've evolved. That end is now but decades away.

The other side of our rite of tragic passage, are roads to happiness. There, we can build the steady state we choose – rising from modernity's ashes. Without those ashes, we can never rise.

****

129

CHAPTER 34 – THE DOUGHNUT WITHOUT COLLAPSE IS A PIPE DREAM

Please don't waste time lobbying governments to think about doughnut economics, or a steady-state economy. If you do, you ask governments to destroy themselves. It's futile.

Instead withdraw consent to their ideology. Withdraw spending from Tesco, Amazon and BP and re-spend people and their skills into existence. Governments live by tweaking a corporate/consumer alliance. To be sure, tax-generated revenue may provide some social infrastructures, but those infrastructures are all oiled to smooth the machinery of corporate and consumer transactions – debt money, retail parks on the ring road…

A steady-state, or doughnut economy will not have monetary capacity for rent. Money flow must not exceed energy flow – that is, the energy of what people can do without fossil fuels. So, by our doughnut, the enclosures must implode – leaving the open common. All property (enclosure) demands rent – land rent, money interest, intellectual property rent and – the elephant in the room – status enclosure – the massive rents demanded by architects, dentists, lawyers, consultants, GPs, corporate "economists" and so on. In short, the doughnut demands the collapse of the middle class. Many who lobby the powers about the doughnut, belong to that class. To have credence to the powers, they must carry enclosed certification – the professorship, the doctorate. Do they know what they do? I think it likely that they can't see the common for the fantasy of their fenced and fortified status.

Anyway, it is plain that to live within the doughnut, will cause the collapse of the casino of rents (including usury), stocks bonds, shares, currencies… In turn, the falling casino will precipitate a cascade of collapsing businesses, causing mass unemployment, collapsing tax revenues and so also of tax-generated "goods" of social care, electricity grids and hard infrastructures. The casino will collapse the economy.

All this will happen anyway. Money markets and debt-created growth, bear no relationship to the real world of soil, people and their skills. The casino is not real. It exists by the faith of punters and by rents pillaged from real economic activity. The pillaged economy has nothing left to give and faith (as witnessed in the middle-class terror of Jeremy Corbyn and Bernie Sanders) is shaky.

It is urgent that we evacuate – that we build durable economic relationships that may emerge more or less intact from beneath the rubble of collapse. It is an epic task. Please engage in it and don't waste energy talking to deaf ears. As you know, extinction of our species and of many more besides, is not far off. Success is the slimmest of slim chances, but all other roads are blocked. Time does not wait.

We can embrace the tragedy of collapse as an essential rite of passage for humanity's coming of age. We'll find a community of species, which have evolved together into the almost infinite complexity of our terrain. That is holy, holy holy! That is interesting. Economies are what people do. Everything we do has a moral, because all actions have consequence. Money is a useful tool, but is a small part of the moral whole. Now, we need, not professors of doughnut economics, telling us what they'd impose. We need a moral awakening, which teaches right and wrong actions. Moral truth is very simple. We came to this mess, because money was enclosed as amoral and so usually, immoral property. Money as personal property is always anti-social. We don't need it. We have each other – leaning to each other's skills – swaying to the music of living time.

****

Moral truth is very simple. Is there any other kind? Well yes, sensual evidence confronts us all the time if we are intelligent to it. Even so, pretty soon, as it enters memory, it gets moralised! That is the purpose of scientific scepticism – to keep ethics at bay, so that sensual evidence (data) may reveal new understanding. The scientist will cultivate a scepticism during her day job, but at leisure she'll re-find her moral self, because everything she does has consequence.

131

It follows that science has no practical use. It lives in an ivory tower. It should remain there unsullied by the goings on of human manipulation and commerce. I value it highly.

Data gathered on CO_2 accumulation, sea level, temperature and so on, leads to new understanding of connections, causes, effects and cycles. The sensual truth of that has been enabled by the sceptical mind. Now, if we enter that understanding into the moral mind of the "scientist", who had previously seen it through her sceptical frame, then her moral outrage must rise and she must surely shake us all severely by the lapels.

There is no conflict between her ivory tower and her moral life. They cohabit side by side. To be effective, the ivory tower must remain unsullied and amoral. To be effective the scientist, as citizen must express her moral outrage. That is not a conflict. It is a kind of binary effectiveness.

Sadly, human ambitions (necessities?) of career and wage have come to mean that "science" is usually far from sceptical and that moral outrage is often in support of entrenched positions, such as theses, schools of thought and the likelihood of peer/career reviews. So called, sceptical science is riddled with commercial, political, and factional polemicists. "Climate" science is at least as corrupted as any other. We can find peer-reviewed papers to support almost anything we think to be to our social, or monetary advantage – GM crops, pesticides, biofuels, coal with CCS, or to the contrary – organic methods, permacultures, earthly limits.

In short, science is riddled with outside influence. We ordinary moral citizens must adopt an automatic scepticism whenever a new "scientific revelation is announced.

We can learn to sieve out those scientists, we can, or can't trust. For myself, there are many "even on my side of arguments" whom I can't trust an inch. There are others, who are rocks.

There is the added complication that many who call themselves scientists, are not – they are technologists – designers of tools. They use the shield of amoral science to justify immoral action. I include medical practice, pharmaceuticals, engineering, economics, architecture and so on. All tools have consequence and so should come with moral justification attached.

132

What on Earth can we do? It's not difficult. Where a tool touches its materials comes a spark of truth. Follow the spark. Learn your trade. *"With usura hath no man a house of good stone – each block cut smooth and well fitting."* But also, congregate in church, temple mosque, pub, library, café. Join the pub chorus round the old Joanna, or raise the lovely vaulted roof with your polyphonic part of Bach, or Palestrina. If you like, you can sing the blues. Rock-and-roll is also good.

Let's make society.

****

CHAPTER 35 – FIRE

It comes down to this, contrary to modernity's dream, "Science" will not save us. The data on CO_2, temperature, sea level and so on, is plain – as is the cause - modernity's way of life. My life must change and only I can change it. We are social creatures – ours is a eusocial evolution – but though much can only change in concert with others, still, I must seek that social change myself, because I am an essential, but tiny part of the whole. I strengthen the whole, or weaken it. There is no neutrality.

How do we live without burning and exploding things? Science will not help. Corporations cannot help without destroying themselves – likewise governments. The only way to discover if we can live without combustion, is to try it. I must attempt to live without fire.

Our species has co-existed with fire from the Palaeolithic. Other hominids (now extinct) too. Now, we must overturn hundreds of thousands of years of evolution. Our adventure is as epic as it sounds. Unless we understand that scale, we shall not succeed. What is required is not a change in government policy, it is a forced overturning of our deepest commons. The common soul of our species must uproot itself from the hearth and resettle a new perception of terrain. That is my and everyone's task.

Those who, since 1990, have jetted to Earth summits to cajole concessions from governments and corporations, have achieved nothing. For myself, I think they have done harm. They have transferred credence to the annual declarations on climate reaction, all of which have ended as empty placation of a restless public – in the eyes of the powers, that is the restless consumer. We must be calmed, or we may slow the currently lucrative pillage of the Earth. Anyway, every year, since 1990, emissions from my way of life have risen unchecked, dipping slightly in recession – and in UK from the collapse of manufacturing – but still, always upwards to oblivion.

No doubt leaders of corporations and their tamed governments will be eager to embrace renewable technologies. They will embrace them and sell them just as they sold oil technologies. They'll be eager to promote their own reading of a green new deal – reaping the cash and launching the same old futurism of electrification of all we do – replacing dirty fossil fuels, with the clean modernity – the quiet hum of progress - of green electricity. Abstract ideas such as governments and corporations are realised by our ballots and purchases. No abstract idea can have a dark night of the soul.

Going back three hundred years, all travel and most manufacturing, apart from ceramics and metalworking, was achieved without fire. But the domestic hearth is another story. It goes back to the very beginnings of homo sapiens. On the other hand, if we travel back only a hundred years (apart from the rail-commuting office worker) all ordinary travel for both work and pleasure was by foot, or bicycle.

Those are simple lessons, when thinking about renewable energy. I think that replacing the domestic hearth and cooking stove – along with light, will use every bit of its possible capacity. Futuristic building-design for solar capture and retention will help in the future, but is no help today. To avoid catastrophic heating (the data is plain) we must act today. Electricity may just (it's a close-run thing) solve the problem of domestic living, but Earth has not capacity to power the family car, aviation, massive shipping, manufacturing. The sequestered photosynthesis of millions of fossilised years has unleashed those things. Now they are set to destroy us. Governments think they can power the same technologies by green energy. They are deluded. We must abandon that whole way of life.

Today, we have urgency, trial and error – not an ideal combination. We need everyone. No governing elites and no corporation will concede to the end of their existence. There are many (NGOs, climate activists...) who'd change the supply side of economic equations – oil extraction and so on. That is futile. We must change the demand – that is, ourselves.

We can evacuate and begin again on solid ground, and hope that this crazy, fire-powered, utterly destructive levitation explodes and falls around us, like lost memories of lost futures. Also falling, like a liberating-confetti onto our passage to new common ground, will be the broken enclosures – the properties, monopolies and schoolings that taught us not to think for ourselves. Now (my old metaphor) where a tool meets its materials is a spark of truth. There and only there, do we receive replies – from a world which may concede to complexity's consensus, and allow our species back into her fold.

****

CHAPTER 36 – BEING, NOTHINGNESS, CUMQUATS AND WALTER SCOTT

So, it comes down to this. The answer to these crazy times, is to evacuate & de-spend the enclosures and to inhabit and re-spend the skill, ingenuity, sensuality (intelligence gathering) and moral probity of the common.

Enclosure desensitises intelligence of our terrains and replaces it with the teachings of enclosed status. There, we will never find the truth. What's more that status has no skills, it is inextricable from discretion, wage, rent, institutional loyalties, schools of thought, and peer/career review. It is set apart from what people do and resides in a sphere of what people say, pay and have become in regards to hierarchy. It has no sense of the climate changing, though it bends to the consensus that climate is changing. The senses (urgency of action) are secondary to the "professed" idea.

Meanwhile, cultures are what people do to make them. A culture is not a state of things. It is a living process – an organism. If you like, it is a gathering of verbs – not nouns. Sensual intelligence of a changing world is harvested by the "actuality of being". Enclosure – that is property – intellectual, land, money and status – resides in a place we may truly call nothingness. (sorry Heidegger).

Currently we ask nothingness to solve the problems of being. That is crazy.

In a wonderful poem about Walter Scott (Green Breeks), Douglas Dunn explores how "professional" people (law, medicine, bank and so on) reside (in their residencies), whereas working people inhabit their slums and cottages. We don't do much in a residence. We do a lot, when we inhabit. Do we want to give further credence to those who reside? Let's inhabit. We inhabit the common, we reside in an enclosure.

By inhabiting, we touch what we inhabit – our gardens, crops, materials, foraging grounds, dew on the grass... They react to us and we to them. Actions and reactions demand both personal morality and communal morality. They also evoke a story, so that we come to inhabit both a mythic sense of how life is and could/should be, and also a wonder at the sensual truth revealed as we tread.

Here is Tony Harrison, from A Cumquat for John Keats.

> It is the cumquat's fruit expresses best, how days have darkness round them like a rind - life a skin of death, which keeps its zest.

Come on, the new middle-class is killing us. There's work to do, which they cannot. Of course, some may say, "Bugger my career, I'm human." Come on and join us.

****

CHAPTER 37 – BIO-MASS, BIO-SPEED AND BIO-ACCELERATION

Yes, as we saw in the last chapter – pursuit of career, kills pursuit of truth. To pursue truth, we must step into wind, sunshine and rain – to which I may add, into famine, flood and storm.

Even so, a walk in the woods, across fields, to the hill-top, along the shore... is a good beginning. To continue the verb metaphor, we will be walking climbing, descending, listening, scenting, touching... Only by that broken twig underfoot, the scent of bluebells, do we find truth. As a farmer, I can see the deepening, or paling of my crops – which indicate accelerating, or decelerating life – that is the mass, energy and velocity of life. Some of those deepenings, or paleings will follow the weather. Often, they may be reactions to my actions – to my appropriate, or inappropriate behaviours. Listen to those reactions. Nobody – no expert opinion, can change that truth. No one is closer to the cycling of life than the farmer. It is tragic that most farmers concede to utterly shallow, career-led academic advice, when true answers are revealed in crop yield (present, past and planned-future) and in messages from the wider ecology, with which they are entwined.

As I step, the Earth responds. Am I a functioning, or at least semi-functioning part of my ecology? Am I appropriate to it, or not? Legends of the Fall, keep hubris at bay. I step along the edge of the Garden and long to be part of a lost terrain. Here's a lesson we can take from our own missteps – Never trust a school of thought entirely, when we cannot even trust ourselves. Also, never, ever trust an institutional consensus. Sometimes we concede to it, to keep our social bonds, but we must know that truth is not involved. We compromise for our companions. Weigh the effects of compromise against the weight of sensual truth. We will have lived that truth and we will have loved our friends. Ridicule brings renegades back to the fold of friendship. As a farmer standing in my guardianship of soil, I can see a whole community of renegades. I am losing friends but cannot return to a renegade fold. I confess, my head is in my hands.

What does zero carbon mean? Truly, zero carbon means extinguishing every man-made fire. Net zero means the gathering of pardons and indulgencies from a fanciful reading of life cycles and then subtracting them from our bad behaviour, to suggest that it is good. People call life cycles, carbon cycles. They are deluded. Life cycles have mass, energy and velocity – the energy being embodied in the mysterious thing we call life. Carbon is simply mass. Nobody, absolutely nobody understands what life is. For our purpose we must call it acceleration due to life – the energy that can transform mass at a variety of speeds. We have energy due to gravity, energy due to sun-light, energy due to sun-heat, energy due to fire, energy due to human labour – which, of course is a very small part of acceleration due to life.

Everyone is measuring mass. Mass is good for pillage. It is good for property. It is (we think) also good to store, like money in a bank. It is dispensation-mass for life's bargaining. We sequester carbon – we think, in quietude – enclosed like a dead idea – a book in a library, which no one needs to bring to life, by their own life – that is by reading it.

But soil life has constantly changing and exchanging velocity, energy and mass. It cannot be sequestered for our peace of mind. It is one and the same with the plants and animals who tread separately to carbon-deluded eyes and with the atmospheric gases, which that whole regulates. Gravity, heat and light make rigid energetic contribution, but living energy and mass cycle at a near infinite varieties of speeds, maintaining and healing the whole.

However, oil, coal and gas were truly sequestered. The word is appropriate. It is not appropriate for soil. The ignition of many millions of fossilised and quietly sequestered years has out-done life's balancing – bringing into the equation both the mass-destructive power of human endeavour – aviation, the family car, centralised distribution, pillage of natural systems, and a surfeit of atmospheric CO_2 – heating ecosystems to beyond their evolutionary range.

140

We must leave the fossils, where they lie, quietly sequestered – also the anaerobic stillness of peat and we must extinguish our bio-fires – timber, oil seeds, sugar-cane, maize, miscanthus.

Earth is heating so fast (Yes, consider time, consider velocity) that we must shrug off our careers and urgently find ways to live as small parts of the biomass and biodiversity of the whole.

We need, not the negative of zero-carbon cultures, but the positive of maximum biomass cultures. As we've seen in previous chapters, an ancient rainforest is a system in balance with an optimum biomass and complexity, which can constantly adjust and heal. It can provide no pardons, or dispensations for destructive human behaviour outside its borders. It can provide no licence to misbehave, stamped with the title – sequestration. But if we attempt to become a part of natural law, so that we also become a part of that optimum biomass – adjusting and healing. then that mass may expand to become more resilient in energy and velocity – which may outweigh (in mass, energy, velocity) the contrary forces, which we call energy due to lifelessness – combustion gases, heat and ashes.

A farm is an organism connected to the organisms of towns. They are one. We call it an agriculture. The farmer, standing in her crops is also a part of universal natural law – in her mind are temperature, wind, rain – the deepening and paling of crops (energy and velocity), networks of roads, rivers and canals to market and from the market (she hopes) "wastes" in return. Differing speeds are everywhere. Time is massive, dangerous, imperative.

We are accelerating towards a lifeless planet. Shouldn't the remedy be obvious?

****

141

CHAPTER 38 – ECONOMY, ECOLOGY – ONE AND INDIVISIBLE

The biomass of Earth is shrinking. It is also weakening. Its immune responses are more and more often overwhelmed by lifeless energy – heat, flood, fire, chainsaw… Lifelessness replaces life – accelerating at tipping points for species after species – the intricate web of those dependent interconnections crumpling before human eyes into memory.

We fully understand what is happening - and why, yet we treat it as part of the "knowledge" we have and do not connect it to our own lives. We devise sophisticated – we think "educated" excuses – sequestration (a convenient untruth) and also humility – It's nice to be humble in the face of the power of time and nature – what can one bloke do?

Yet it is the sum of singular people who make up the whole of the species. The species can only mutate its behaviour, by the adaption of individuals. One bloke can mutate. Every bloke (sexless term) can mutate the species. There is no other way, because the sensual intelligence of the species, always – I mean always – must pass through the senses of individuals. There are commons of good behaviour, which bind us, but human sensuality is mine and mine alone.

Anyway, we face The Great Sickening on two fronts – of nature and of society.

All "developed" economies will now collapse – the weight and energy of applied ideas (lifelessness), outweighs the weight and energy of what people do to grow food and distribute it, to build and maintain houses and so on. The energy; the vitality of the verb to do is outweighed and out-forced by the contrary power of status, that is, of the noun, enclosure. The effects of enclosure include rent for the abstract properties of status, land, ideas and money (interest is rent). The abstract outweighs the real and bleeds it.

We also have debt-created money – that is debt-created abstract property.

Economic collapse is inevitable.

Then, to massively add to the power of lifelessness and the sickening of life, we have a second front - the sudden release of millions of years of sequestered photosynthesis, which both thickens the blanket of atmospheric CO_2 and magnifies the destructive powers of human hubris. Great forests fall before it and human ego is so puffed up by that prowess, that it devises poisons – pesticides, fungicides, herbicides to remove every form of life apart from a few selected crop species and a few pretty garden trees and flowers.

The collapse – the imploding of life on Earth, is inevitable.

How do we restore sickening economies back to health?

How do we restrain ourselves from poisoning, felling and suffocating our living Earth? We cannot say, how do we restore the health, mass and vitality of natural systems? Natural systems themselves must achieve that. We can only say, how do we return health to human economies, so that they and their wider ecologies become one, vital – regenerative – healthy?

How do we undo what we have done? Of course, we cannot. It was done yesterday. We are not time travellers.

We ride the present and cannot jump off. No future ingenuity will save us. In truth, the future will bear our present effect.

Plainly we must descend from those abstract, yet destructive ideas of property and so on and inhabit sensual reality of the present. The present is the unknown. Who's for the ride?

That simple idea is heresy to most. It embodies what should be self-evident – economy and ecology are one and indivisible. Even so we walk along the edge of the Garden, looking in dreamily from our fields and towns. We cannot enter. All agriculture disrupts what it has replaced.

So, how do we minimise disruption so that at least we maintain the freedom to dreamily gaze? The Garden must massively expand and human effects must massively shrink. Then, the health of the whole may be enough to begin the healing.

One lesson is that human economies must collapse. We cannot "green" their current form, because they currently have no form – they have anti-form, like anti-matter. The abstract bleeds the real, sucking it into the hands of property (an idea), leaving the living, breathing species on the edge (it cannot be denied) of oblivion.

"The health of soil, plant, animal, man is one and indivisible". That has been the central principle for organic methods since the days of the early pioneers in the 1940's. I think that instruction is also much older. Incidentally, organic does not define a state – a noun. It lives in a world of verbs, of what we do. It describes a method.

Here is Lawrence Woodward, who has been a rock in the storm of market opportunists, who ship-wrecked the true organic movement thirty years ago. It needs revival.

> *At the moment we cannot be definitive on how to farm for health or how to make health infectious. We do not know what the important transmission factors are or how the "mutuality of actions" work – whether through micro-organisms, bacteria, energy, vitality, self – organisation or something else?*

> *However, we do know there are some things which are likely to be important and which farmers should pay attention to; these revolve around managing the soil and above and below ground livestock through biological system management and not through inputs whether these are synthetic or organic.*

"Whether these are synthetic or organic" – Yes, if we consider the organism of farm, or town, those organic imports diminish the organic mass and vitality of the terrain from which they are imported. How do we maintain the health – the metabolism, of our own farm, village, town. without that social injustice? You see, where ecology and economy become one is our goal. A balance of ecology also requires the equity of social systems.

They are one and indivisible.

Once again, we return – enclosure (property) defines a state. States do nothing. We lie in state by bleeding the common. The common is dynamic. It defines good behaviour – rations of what we can do and of what we can have and it guides what we do both together and in our terrains.

LIFEBOATS AND LANDFALL

Developed economies are intrinsically destructive and because of their size they cannot be greened. They embody a destructive way of life. Our only choice is to evacuate that economy and to live a different way of life.

De-growing what is destructive is no remedy – it remains destructive.

A green New Deal for what is destructive may shrink its ill-effects, but it will also remain destructive.

But anyway, de-growth will fail as a strategy, even towards that limited end because –

As we've seen, de-growth of monetarist economies, will not only diminish their ill effects, it will destroy them. Growth is essential to developed economies. Money-flow must accelerate, but the physical economy of labour and resources is shrinking.

Sooner, or later, the rope will break. Collapse is inevitable.

If collapse is inevitable, we must choose it as necessary – as an essential step. If (Brian Davey's metaphor) shipwreck is inevitable tomorrow, we'd be wise to launch the lifeboats today.

So, my chosen first step is not of collapse and retreat to my bunker, it is to launch the lifeboats and to colonise what we find at landfall, leaving as small a footprint as we can manage. Collapse will loom darkly over us like a prophecy, but a little delay will give us time to settle. As, we've seen in our chapter Being, Nothingness, Cumquats and Walter Scott, we must inhabit rather than reside. Our habits must mingle with those of the other species we find. In the past, the word colonial has meant bloody invasion, pillage and the construction of over-seeing residencies. Now it must be different.

We shall inhabit, which will prove a delight. How do we know the habits of other species, without study and without the physical trial and error of our own habits? Every individual must be involved.

We shall receive no instruction from the residences.

When collapse comes – sooner is best for the planet – later is best for our infant plans – we can hope that our colonies are resilient enough to welcome refugees aboard and so expand into new terrain – becoming stronger.

The farm is the perfect place for learning that habitation. It is also the perfect place (where better?) for moral philosophy. Farmers are currently the luckiest people on Earth. The farm is the core of agricultural economies (towns, roads, cities). It is the primary source. If we can properly inhabit our farms and also properly inhabit those roads to and from market (both at the farmer's fingertips) we can have a glimmer of a chance for whole societies to *healthily inhabit* their rations of Earth. Remember that economics is just one branch, though probably the stoutest branch, of moral philosophy.

A contagious moral philosophy which is rooted in our habitations – our families, skills and terrains - could infuse the common course of things and shrug off the phantasies of those who pillage and reside. Remember morality tells us what to do – how to behave well. It is a living force.

At their chore (removing the cults and hierarchies) Christianity, Islam, Hinduism, Buddhism, Taoism, Confucianism, all say the same.

As just about every "green" writer of substance says (it's a long list), a moral awakening is our final life-belt for rescue from a sea of colonial residencies tossing wildly on waves of their own making – the consumer consumed by the consumed.

****

CHAPTER 39 – OUR HABITATION

How do we re-settle? By trial & error. But here are some thoughts. Every habitation must begin with some sort of understanding and some sort of a plan.

Potatoes contain about 80% water

Carrots contain 90%

Cereals contain 15%

A tonne of potatoes contains 200kg of nutrients

A tonne of carrots contains 100kg

A tonne of cereals contains 850 kg (dried in the field by sunshine)

That is why cereals have founded towns and cities. They are very light for transport. A ship's hold can carry 4.25 more nutrients than potatoes. Differing types of bread have been the staple of most cultures.

Cereals and potatoes contain very similar nutrients.

We would not be very well if we consumed a diet entirely of cereals. That has created a chronic (sometimes acute) sickness of the poor in many parts of the world. So, most fruit, roots and leaves are best grown close to home. Without engine oil, that thought is essential.

There is much demonisation of cereals, but not much sign that people can resist a hot loaf, straight from the oven, a flat bread straight from the griddle, or hold back their pride in the local pasta. A loaf of bread, a jug of wine and thou.

Cereals can be traded between regions, as scarcity and surplus demand. In my dreams (reality is very close) small sailing vessels of 500 tonnes (they are coming to fruition as we speak) will prove ideal (along with river/canal boats and barges) for that trade – or indeed, sometimes for that rescue mission. 2,000 tonne vessels will soon follow. That's a lot of grain – bearing in mind our primary aim will be to localise. *

Cereals are useful both in time and space (tonnage). They can be transported not only through scarcity and surplus of regions and neighbours, but also between scarcity and surplus of hard, or abundant times. They can be stored for years. They will remain central to our harvest festivals!

I begin with a defence of cereals, because they give emergency leeway to otherwise localised food systems – of course, the bulk of our cereal crops will also be consumed locally – or within a town/mill/terrain relationship.

Cuba successfully rode the oil blockade by diminishing the contribution of large collective farms and by encouraging citizens to both "grow their own" and to form small grower co-operatives – the organiponicos. At landfall, we can do the same – vegetable and fruit growing can weave into town – into private gardens and public spaces – derelict car parks for instance, or roadside avenues of fruit trees. Quite literally, hope can sprout from beneath paving stones. Meanwhile, market gardens, orchards and dairies can ring those towns, occupying, and revitalising the oil-desolation of retail park and ring road.

The same will happen in Suburbia as it re-centralises into villages and small towns sat in a sea of biomass - what we currently separate as agriculture and horticulture. Is the distinction any use for our new adventure? I think not. As man-power replaces oil-power, all arable farmers will be forced into a more horticultural mind-set. Mixed farmers will be forced into both a more horticultural and also, a more "dog and stick" mind-set.

Fields will shrink into the compass of man-power, with the additional advantage of attention to detail – the intelligence of many more senses. Large collective farms have not worked well in history. In private ownership, they'd become the now familiar colonial plantation owner and his hundreds – even thousands of slaves. In public ownership, they'd become institutionalised and wooden. Our new settlers will not stand for either. They'll want to use their own senses and their own brains.

With all this shrinking, you say, you are shrinking back in time and towards low yields and inefficiency. No, I say we are shrinking back into a world without fossil fuel and biofuels. We must put out the fires. We cannot have massive tractors and their massive machinery. We replace them with people – the ingenuity, dexterity and sensuality of very many people. To fully utilise people, it must be an egalitarian landfall.

I'd say that most work done today is not only futile, it is destructive – insurance, banking, advertising, market research, manufacture of useless shiny things; of cars, trucks, aeroplanes. We scurry to destroy ourselves. Those many millions engaged in destruction can instead be engaged in useful production. Eventually, as the hard work of transition passes, people will have far, far more leisure time without oil, as they had with it.

There will be work reviving canal and navigable river systems and small harbours all around the coastline. There will be work building the new sail-trading ships and smaller craft and there will be work on the farm and with rural housing – plus new tool-makers, weavers, millers...

I say we cannot have fossil fuels, or biofuels, but anaerobic digestion is different. Fermentation is everywhere. It is essential to the continuation of life. It happens anyway. Harvesting gas is rather like hunter-gathering. We anaerobically ferment agricultural and household "waste" and use the gas. We exchange one gas for another and use the energy. CO_2 for methane seems a good idea. Tiny digestors may provide for the domestic stove. Farm digestors may provide for some small machinery. Neighbouring farms may share that machinery, for initial cultivation perhaps - and what about a combine harvester – used for only 1 month every year – travelling between farms.

I am talking low horse-power. The scything, stooking, stacking and threshing could be done by hand. In difficult weathers the combine harvester can dash between rain-storms. It's a pleasant thought.

Another thought – ceramics and metal working (re-purposing) need considerable heat. The digestor may provide it. We shall only know if it can, by trial, error and rationing – that is by fair distribution. Bear in mind the end is to shrink our impact on both climate and ecology, so that we cannot grow crops for the digestor, we can only place it as a part of the cycles of use and return.

How do we minimise our impact? My own remedy is to think of human cultures occupying glades in the larger forest, rather than the permacultural remedy of imitating the canopies and understories of the forest. I think we can grow a greater biomass in the glade – one that meets our needs in a smaller space, while around us, the wilds can expand. We'll only learn by doing it. Certainly, my crop of wheat needs full sun. Why do I say remedy? – because our culture is currently very sick and will not survive.

****

* https://ecoclipper.org/

CHAPTER 40 – DOG AND STICK

How do we extract crops, while maintaining future yields? – By cycles of use and return, but also by introducing generative phases in rotation. Perennial cropping of fruit and nut trees and bushes is useful and perennial cereal prairies as dreamed by the Land Institute may be a thing of the future. Nevertheless, even perennial cereals will need regenerative phases – by either cutting and mulching, or by grazing.

A very old rule of thumb is one year of cropping to two years of pasture (once called fallow). Many organic growers, practice two years of cropping to four years of green manure, or pasture.

I don't see how we can escape that simple rule. I think a vegan rotation could work very well, but I think the introduction of animals would work better. Meat, eggs and dairy add to the diversity of both biomass in the field and to the quality of diet.

Used as part of rotation, animals increase the final yield. Pasture and green manure work equally well, so that animals add to overall harvested biomass, rather than being (as is commonly cited) an extremely inefficient way to grow food.

If efficient growing systems do best by imitating natural cycles, then that sort of proportion of animals is surely appropriate.

Of course, we cannot have feed-lots, broiler houses, battery houses and piggeries, but also how much area can we dedicate for perennial grasslands dedicated solely to dairy, beef and sheep production? Think of a glade in the forest, dedicated to human cultures. How big can that glade be, to avoid collapsing eco-systems and swelling atmospheric CO_2?

All agriculture disrupts the natural system it has replaced (my mantra). How much of the natural must re-grow and how far must human interference shrink? Whatever the grassland polemicists say

– no (UK) grassland is as rich in life as the forest it has replaced. Yet, beautiful human cultures have evolved with grasslands. How can we deny that?

Here's something – thinking of the UK, those wide upland pastures were not created by ingenious local habits. They are not an ancient cynefin, terroir, or clan territory, they are the result of a vicious aristocratic (most of it) expulsion of people from their lands. The enclosures were a land grab for the currency of sheep's wool. A very few got rich, nearly all ended in starvation, city slums, or in voyaging Atlantic, or Pacific oceans.

Close cropped uplands are nearly deserted - economically but for widely-scattered farmsteads and ecologically, but for sheep, crow, buzzard, a few skylarks, curlews and so on and of course tourists – who may be the largest economic contributor – along with farm subsidy and the meagre lamb trade. The tourists come for the wide, desolate spaces and think it wild.

But those scattered farmsteads could surely find a better living in re-foresting and re-wilding? We certainly need timber more than we need sheep. We also need to overturn the terrible injustice of the enclosures and bring people and life back to those places. Those farmsteads can still provide lamb for local butchers and (if soil permits) milk to local dairies.

Today, the wool trade says that upland wool is wiry & useless – only suited to carpet-making. But don't we like carpets? The old fulling and weaving mills can return from dereliction. People can widen their skills into forestry and wood-working and bring new meaning to the word cynefin. Eighty per cent of Welsh lamb is exported. Well, eighty per cent of that land area can certainly be re-wilded, or re-forested without the smallest economic harm. Eighty per cent is a precarious percentage.

Thinking of pastured flocks and herds, the East of the country is in desperate need of them for its tired and half-dead soils, while the West has far too many. Is that a recipe for a beautiful friendship, which also increased the species diversity of both West and East? Also, bear in mind that we'll not need the vast acreage of cereals, previously destined for animal feed. Economies will gain some slack. Also, efficient, most ecologically-integrated flocks and herds will follow, not the grain market, but the seasons. People will re-learn the true calendar (UK) of Spring, Summer, Autumn and Winter. Communities may synchronise with the true movement of time. Each month will contain ecologic/economic meaning. That is a delight.

****

CHAPTER 41 – A SHORT BUT TANGLED TRAGI-COMIC PLOT

Each month will contain ecologic/economic meaning. For us – for developed economies – all of which are agricultures, or dependent on agricultures – that meaning will contain a large thought-stifling smog of tragedy. We think we cannot do what is right, because of the tragedies our action will cause.

The central premise of all I write is that we must embrace tragedy – that there is no other course, but to take the tragic rite of passage towards the light on the other side. Our ways of life are causing terrible tragedies. It is illogical to say that we cannot act out remedies, because of the tragedies they'd cause to our tragedy-causing ways of life.

For me, another essential mantra, is that comedy and tragedy share identical plots – the one of mind - the other of heart. Of course, as we see in the best writing and hear in the best and deepest music, comedy and tragedy can weave together as one – just as heart and mind are one.

> It is illogical to say that we cannot act out remedies, because of the tragedies they'd cause to our tragedy-causing ways of life. – Is that not the archetype for the best stage comedies and tragedies?

Of course, we could also say, it is illogical to say that we cannot act out remedies, because of the ridicule and laughter they'd draw from those still engaged in ridiculous ways of life.

That last applies to most of peer-dependent, career-dependent academia and in particular to "climate science".

It applies to me in conversation with friends and family – I am ridiculous to some and dangerously tragic to others. Usually I draw back – accepting the role of clown and resenting the role of darkness! My life is entangled with theirs. I've no wish to disentangle. How on Earth do we disentangle from our common tragedy, together? One thing I know, is that I've only partially disentangled myself.

****

CHAPTER 42 – *JONGLEURS DE JOIE*, OR PROPHETS OF DOOM

Supressing the tragedy and enjoying the comedy, seems a profitable course. Remember that reality – the plot – is the same for both. Taking the tragic road to the light on the other side is the same as taking the comic road. The roads are the same.

Comedy is of the mind – we do need the mind – we need a quick wit and quick responses. Releasing too much of the heart to public gaze aggrandises us as heroes of noble tragedy – and apart. Comedy makes us ridiculous, but included. Truly, whole societies – indeed the species herself are ridiculous. Laughter brings us together.

Tragedy can bring us together in laughter. As we leave the oil machinery behind – evacuate the enclosures and settle the common – we must first pass through tragedies, which we ourselves have made - well, tragic-comedy. Let's be *jongleurs de joie*; lords (and subjects) of misrule; Don Quixote as Everyman (sexless). If laughter defeats the tears, we'll have a glimmer of a chance.

Those seriously engaged in maintaining suicidal ways of life – that is, nearly everybody – will label us comic. Keep the label and keep throwing it back. Might we not eventually fall in a common heap of helpless laughter?

Never forget that seriousness is a biological catalyst – an enzyme, which extinguishes thought. It is the puffing up of authority in the face of danger - the posturing of rival animals. Many species use it to extinguish sensuality and fear. Those serious peer-reviewed articles, or newspaper editorials use posture (seriousness) as a replacement for thought – just as rival silver-backs swell with stupidity to achieve their status.

Seriousness proposes "realistic" responses to the ecological, economic and climatic cliff edge – that is, it shuts off the problem and swells with stupidity. It cannot not listen to truly reasonable voices, because it has blocked its ears.

Perhaps it is true that we have but three ways of seeing – the tragic, the comic and the serious.

We can escape neither the first, nor the second, but the third – seriously?

****

CHAPTER 43 – AND LIKE THIS INSUBSTANTIAL PAGEANT FADED

My time on this little podium is ending and the book will close. What remains is the "actuality of being" – each heartbeat unique, becoming instant memory. Yet that actuality is outside time because it is constant and yet is the embodiment of time, because its actuality is that mysterious thing – life herself – the only conduit of experience. As we've said, it is being.

Past, future and this book's advice are nothingness. Being is the essential verb in a midden of nouns.

Life is common sense. Common sense is the measure of everything. It is what mystics from every culture have called timelessness – through veils of Maya and clouds of unknowing...

We *Jongleurs de Joie* can celebrate it, while the powers, who seek to mutate past illusions into future illusions must supress it. The "actuality of being" must be supressed (at all costs) by schools, universities and newspaper editorials. Life is the absolute lord of misrule.

That divide could be the ancient divide between church (ancestor worship, animism, polytheism and even monotheism) and the state. In history (and in guessed pre-history) the state (clan, tribe, family – even city-state) has usually been subject to a common, both spiritual and pragmatic vision. Now we have the opposite. Everywhere, church and state are becoming one. In other words, the church has been colonised by the state.

In more recent history, church and state have restrained each other into some sort of a balance of morality and amorality.

Listen – I attend no church, or temple and cannot say many of the things required of me, to belong in those communities. I fit the label of atheist.

Yet I think – no believe – that a common spiritual and pragmatic vision, is our last hope to evacuate the suicidal consensus of the powers. We cannot outstate the state, but we can out-believe it.

Only a common sense of being can outweigh the nothingness.

As Siegfried Sassoon said, surfacing from the deep trauma of an idiotic war – This is from memory, because I can't find the book. Like much in life, the spine has fallen off –

"It is only from the inner-most silences of the heart, that we know the world for what it is, and ourselves for what the world has made us."

****

CHAPTER 44 – OUR WOUNDED EARTH. WHO HOLDS THE KNIFE?

Climate is disbalancing faster than all predictions. Tipping points come and nudge still others – accelerating. Plainly, no one has a clue, but this – it is our doing and we must undo it. And we don't need to understand that vast complexity. We never have and never will. But we do understand what we've done to cause it. It is our way of life and the number of people living it.

Let's also get this straight, most people in the world are not guilty. They have no car, they've never flown, they do not ask for much. They survive on the smallest patches of soil. Those people should be our model. Professor Kevin Anderson has been an incorruptible rock in all the excuses and dispensations. Consult him for an excellent collection of statistics. Why receive them second hand?

However, as a farmer, along with most practical people, I know many things that the institutions do not. I know why the predictions of IPCC and so on, have been wildly and dangerously optimistic.

Firstly, the sequestration figures, which are entered into the modelling are grossly overstated – to my eyes they are outright fiction. Farmers can measure sequestration rates, season by season, by the very simple measure of crop yields. They can correlate those figures with what they have done to achieve them – the husbandry failures, or successes, adverse weathers and so on. Bear in mind that biomass yield also indicates photosynthetic potential and that yield also indicates soil fertility, which along with plant biomass, climate physicists call sequestration. Up until the 1970s, and the world over, such data was copiously collated and analysed by countless "agricultural colleges" and government ag department. It remains archived, but unread.

From over fourty-years' experience, I can say that the utmost an agricultural system can achieve is balance and that balance is rare.

Close enough is a good aspiration. We cannot "draw down" further carbon. Agricultures always disrupt the natural systems they replace.

Moreover, I place this pigeon among the cats, to say that natural systems too can only achieve balance, though that balance will have a greater biomass than a well-managed field, or garden. Total biomass will fluctuate by a complexity of injury (such as fire) and repair, but it can never sequester more biomass and energy than the limiting finity of its soil volume, water and so on.

So, natural systems replenish after injury (as in agricultural rotation), but will always end in balance within the physical boundaries of soil and ultimately of Earth herself. We cannot say that sufficient acreage of ancient woodland will "draw down" a proportion of the "carbon" emitted from an adjoining human economy. That economy must deal with its own ill-effects. An ancient rainforest can provide nothing as dispensation to excuse indulgence-seeking human cultures.

IPCC and most other projections only work (along with the futurism of my next point), because they add the dispensation of "good" natural systems to compensate for the ill-behaviour of humans. In other words, sequestration modelling is fiction. It is a vast and deadly fiction. It is tragic that most of the green movement has embraced it as dispensation for unchanged behaviour. Einstein would be horrified, but something else is missing from our climate physicist's calculations - She otherwise thinks of energy, but in natural systems she measures only mass – matter. Where are energy (vitality) and time (velocity) in her calculations? She accepts that matter and energy always remain in some form or other, yet in sequestration figures, she conveniently forgets it. In short, to a farmer, she is plain bonkers. Our climate physicist measures the nouns and forgets the verbs.

Secondly, what humans have done to cause climate-heating they must now undo. We can save ourselves, by changing ourselves, but nothing else can. Time is very, very short. Net emissions are a fantasy.

This has a series of points, which are really one and the same.

a. We cannot change a political system by argument within the accepted boundaries of its beliefs. Thus we give credence to the beliefs. Jeremy Corbyn has been the only politician of recent times, to challenge the UK political system. He was swiftly "dealt with". However, he remains a much-admired figure. Therein is a clue.

b. We cannot change what we've come to call industrialisation, using its own tools. The tools are the culture. We don't change industrialisation, we find new (or old) tools to create a new culture.

c. Giant corporations exist by our purchases – of oil, airline tickets, cars, food commodities, from grain to bananas. If we think giant corporations are a problem, we don't remove the problem by lobbying corporations to behave better. Instead, we withdraw consent. We remove our spending and re-spend it elsewhere. Improving corporate supply techniques continues our dependence on corporate supply – and gives it credence. The answer is to remove the corporation from our culture. This could be very easily done if people find a common ethic to withdraw their money and replace it as they choose. The corporation thinks the consumer is king by both following and creating consumer "trends". The corporation will more than happily "green" its tools. Trends are where the money lies. What we ask, they will do. But the corporate model is the problem. We, the grower, baker, miller, weaver, sailor... must take back the tools.

d. Michael Moore's film, The Planet of the Human, paints the picture very well. That it hits the problem with a sledge hammer is probably also appropriate. But the film needed a postscript, or perhaps a part two. What do we do when the sledge hammer has crumbled the whole "thing" into its original aggregate? Who first used the term "the thing" – I think it may have been William Cobbet? Anyway, I've encountered the phrase several times in books I've enjoyed, from the Nineteenth Century and perhaps earlier. We all know what it means and the thing's original aggregate will need some re-purposing. The film's target was industrialised green energy. I support the sledge hammer. But, in doing so it attacked all green energy. That is either an oversight, or a mistake.

For very many centuries local engineers and blacksmiths have made ingenious wind pumps and mills. There is good reason to think that such pumps and mills could be adapted to power turbines for electricity. Hydro power is still more ancient and farm-scale, village scale – even perhaps, town-scale hydro turbines could easily be constructed by such village-scale labour and ingenuity.

What the film calls the elephant in the room – intermittency - could (and should), like seasons, day and night, be embodied in the culture as a simple law of nature. Something we doubly value, when we've got it, and accept when we haven't. We store food through Winter. Currently no one has a genuine solution to storing wind electrical energy for windless days, or hydro energy in drought. Like everything in life, we can have a ration. Our new culture can manage that ration fairly, like irrigation in the Mediterranean, or medieval strip fields, by laws of the commons. A re-entry of time, seasons and rationing into a common vision of how things are, would prove both a beautiful and useful addition to our economic behaviours.

Our own farm exports a little more electricity than it imports by a small wind turbine (rated 6kw) and solar panels (rated 4kw). I can see no reason why my son, who is a good welder, could not build the structure of such a turbine (blades, tower, bearings), entirely from scrap materials (the aggregate). He'd have to study a bit more to make the turbine, but certainly someone in our village community could – and entirely from the "aggregate" of lost industrialisation. The farm's electricity demand includes the welder, fridges and freezers for our butchery and a high demand at apple-pressing time (September to January) for apple mill, hydraulic press and pasteurisers. We have an electric grain mill and of course an ordinary domestic demand (from an old, cold, stone farmhouse). We burn wood for heat. Something we must somehow stop.

Perhaps solar voltaic is doomed. I haven't the knowledge to know. Currently, I, or my sons cannot make a solar panel. We could however, easily make a solar thermal system and we could also make a bio-digester for farm "wastes" – returning the "digestate" to the soil. Our aerobic composting system is less efficient, releasing an equal amount of uncaptured gas to the air and of uncaptured heat to the surrounding environment. In a better future we could certainly capture that heat – bearing in mind that most of the heat will be produced in winter, when heat is needed.

Heat pumps – particularly ground-source heat pumps could similarly be constructed by local ingenuity, from local "aggregate", and as a good way to use what electricity we have, bearing in mind the limits of wind and rain.

We need to live in much smaller, cheaper houses, built for "solar gain". At the moment, few of us do. Changing housing is a mountain to climb, but must be an essential part of the utopian vision, which is the only vision to draw us back from the environmental and climatic cliff edge we peer over. The vertigo is freezing our actions - as is dependency. Utopia can be a common goal. Few will dispute its truth – but most shrug it off as impracticable. I say utopia is essential – we must always compromise utopia – not our previously failed utopian compromise. Instead, having failed, we re-focus again on that perfected vision and then discover a new compromise. The least-worst option is the best option.

Direct traction from tide, gravity (hydro) and wind has been long tried and tested. It may still be the best option for mills and manufactories. It is easily devised by local ingenuity and labour.

The direct traction of sail power is almost universally ridiculed. I've no idea why. We'll still need to trade scarcity and surplus and I think, happiness – that is beautiful things and experiences, unique to their terrains. Without sail power we descend into the brutalist side of localism. Why be brutal? (apologies to beautiful brutes). That's another thing – wonder at the beauties of nature and despair at our clumsy footsteps, is another essential catalyst (or rather, enzyme) for the good.

Utopia is certainly possible, but we know it is unlikely. The whole – every species in nature - is the same – healing wounds – finding a balance and then, repairing new wounds. Homo sapiens is (should be) just the same. Earth as a whole, is the same. We can liberate both personal and community sensuality – and the intelligence of those senses. We can cast off the fictions of the powers. Even if we fail, because that cliff edge is just too close for the time that remains, we can know that our road was the road to happiness. We must pass through economic tragedy. Collapse is inevitable. We cannot tell if we will emerge the other side, but we can hope so.

****

164

CHAPTER 45 – THE DARK

That my reality of collapsing ecosystems and catastrophic climatic disbalance is not the reality of anyone I meet, is driving me into the dark. I do not know how long I can endure total isolation. I may not emerge at all. And my "on-line" contacts seem, but for the fingers of one hand, as unreal as my neighbours and friends. The most august "climate scientists" treat climate heating as an abstract idea, the nuances of which bring them to heated discussions with their peers – who form themselves into schools of thought. That's how they spend their days. To them, climate projections are abstract ideas made real, while their climate-collapsing lives remain real, but relatively insignificant. The real destructive force of their lives is outweighed by their own abstract solutions to that destruction. So, they subconsciously decide that their lives must go on unchanged, and also that arguments about solutions should also go on unchanged. An academic career in climate change, becomes more important than the climate change itself.

Similarly, academics create models for steady-state, circular, or doughnut economies and, because of their status (doctorate, professorship) present their findings to governments and corporations. It's nice to move in such circles.

Not one of those economists has courage to accept that any of those solutions would cause total economic collapse – mass unemployment, crashing tax revenues and so collapsing social and hard infrastructures.

A steady state economy is one we can adopt, only after collapse. Indeed, collapse is essential to their birth. Any future must first embrace the deep tragedy of collapse, before re-building can begin.

No economist that I've encountered is brave enough to profess that truth. Instead, they speak in the language that the powers will understand – that is, in nice, little, spun illusions.

There is no way out from our predicament than tragedy. I can embrace that. It is the unreality, which kills.

Satellite imagery will record no difference before and after collapse – roads, bridges, harbours, towns, hills, woods and fields will all remain the same.

That is our destination – changed people – same Earth.

****

CHAPTER 46 – CHANGED PEOPLE, SAME EARTH

Our destination – changed people, same Earth. People know how to behave (to travel) by inner moral guidance, or otherwise by coercion by other people. That coercion is sometimes violent; sometimes seductive.

The only way to change myself is to discover a new moral guidance, and if we are coerced, to shrug off that coercion.

That discovery must always be solitary – even though common circumstance may provoke a discovery, which is side by side and in common with others. We have evolved together and are likely to discover together - simultaneously and similarly.

I think it best if we think of education as coercion. Certainly, it has done our current culture real harm. We'll find only dead hierarchies and status monopolies there. Those who say, education is the answer would but propagandise their point of status and superior view.

Is this little piece forcing my point of view? – perhaps, but I hope not. I say, find your own point of view – your own intelligence, received through your own senses of both our lovely Earth and of the prevailing human cultures, which are palpably set on destroying our only possible home.

How do we behave at home? How do we manage that economy? How do we define and ration both chores and pleasures – both in what we can have and in what we can do? How would we like family members to behave together? Then, further afield, how would we like our friends and neighbours to behave? I think, we'd think of rationing – of fair shares of both actions (liberties and restraints) and of things, for instance, of food – fairly breaking bread.

If everybody answered those basic economic questions in those filial micro economies, then the macro economies of village, parish, town and nation state would function more happily and more appropriately – knit to both specific behavioural terrains and to the wider terrain.

The same goes for the microcosm of each trade – each with specific skills and perceptions, which contribute to the whole.

Education destroys the lot. The corporation destroys the lot. Enclosure (property) destroys the lot. That's my little coercion.

Morality guides what we do. Cultures are made up by what people do. Cultures are not what we have, or have achieved, they are always what we do.

A fine painting, or piece of music - a beautiful building, or ingenious machine are usually what ancestors did. We admire their doing. When we enter a fine piece of music, we enter that perhaps ancient doing. We re-embody our ancestor. We remain active. We have not entered a thing, or a possession. We re-live an experience. Afterwards, we say, what a marvellous experience it was re-living that marvellous ancestor's life. If during, our musical experience, we let ourselves intrude, because we are weary for some reason, or because we cannot restrain our critical faculty, then we will have spoiled the experience. We will not have lived it. It will be despoiled - despoiled by a held opinion or status quo.

In truth, the finest art, from a simple folk song to a complex string quartet, becomes so, only when the composer's temporal identity has gone and she has become Everyman. She does not express herself. She will have taken the living roll of ancestors, who similarly sang. She is the living act of the culture as a whole. Most of us instinctively know that if an artist says that she is breaking boundaries, or that her warrior spirit is trampling old hallowed ground – we know that she is ephemeral ambition – trite fashion seeker.

A culture is a collective of methods – of tools. States kill methods.

The purpose of enclosure is to kill the method and assert the new state – that is the new property, rent, class, copyright holder.

The purpose of the common is to continue, but regulate (like a sluice) the flow of what people can do to live fairly by each other and appropriately in their terrains, so that descendants have the undiminished means to live in a similar way. The evolved advice of ancestors, who provided for the present, is usually revered. Ancestors have the advantage that they level us all.

The past creates the present, just as the present creates the future. Without a common rationing, the future will suffer. That suffering is a betrayal of ancestors. It is a deep shame. Without such commons, we have chaos. The songbird who delights us today, as we excavate another acre of her habitat, will only be gone in the future. Today, we pause and listen. The silence comes a year, or two later.

We have chaos. We have status, property, status law and property law. We have usury and rent. We have enlightened futuristic education, which denies the present – and relentless enclosure-journalism. We have no future.

Please step down into the wind, sunshine and rain of the common. Consider how you'd like your children to behave, then follow suit. Don't follow Great Thunberg and the school strikers. Reassuringly take their hands at last, for that is what they ask. Then, together turn away from the crumbling cliff edge, until we all find fertile ground to inhabit – making tools, which are at last adapted, as best we can, to its ways.

****

CHAPTER 47 – SUMMARY OF THE WORLD ACCORDING TO A NOBODY

By the act of withdrawing our spending from the enclosures, and replacing it in the common we play our part in the collapse of enclosure and the revival of the common.

We cannot prevent collapse of the enclosures, but we can create scattered economies durable enough to emerge from the ashes of modernity. At least 70% (guess) of those scattered economies must be made up of money-less activity and because, without enclosure, we shall have no property; no rent; no debt; no casino - the mass and energy of money need be very, very small, relative to today.

As Adam Smith says, Money can have no purpose, besides purchasing goods, but goods can have many purposes, besides purchasing money. Adam Smith's thoughts on economy are identical to David Fleming's (the slack economy). In both, money is a tool, but cannot be "capital".

If necessary, (bad harvests, for instance) we can put aside that tool of exchange and instead rely on the exchanged energy of people.

It seems a long time ago that Richard Douthwaite introduced me to this thought – money-flow should not exceed energy-flow. Energy-flow is the power of what people do. Recently, the power of what people do, has been magnified by fossil fuels by thirty or fourty times over (another wild guess).

It is plain that merely removing fossil fuels from our culture will cause monetary collapse and so also inevitably, economic collapse.

On top of that, enclosed commons of land, status, ideas and money have created these various irresponsible properties (home as castle). I mean land, bank account, doctorate & so on) – all of which charge large rents. When I take my £10 per hour to pay for the solicitor's £300 per hour, the £290 difference is rent for the property of monopoly status. Interest is rent for the property of money and so on. *

So, fossil-fuelled money-flow has been vastly increased by enclosure - by rent collection from the probity of the real economy by an irresponsible, libertarian enclosure. Today, very few commons remain. If we like, we can exchange property (to liven things up) in a casino of stocks, bonds, shares and currencies.

Of course, collapse of an "economy" whose foundation is irresponsibility is inevitable, but the slightest prick to that casino fervour will immediately prick the faith of punters and so, the whole "thing" will cascade (pack of cards really is the appropriate metaphor).

David Fleming's metaphor is bloke falls off bicycle when forward motion no longer holds him upright.

But here's a thing – a moneyless economy survives on the common and it survives everywhere by means of the household - in family values and in rations of both what we can have (toys, food...) and in what we can do (chores and pleasures). That economy extends into groups of friends, clubs, common interest societies, pub sing-songs, churches, meeting houses, mosques, temples, synagogues – in conversation with a stranger, exhilarated at the view from a hill top – in festivals and holidays ...

So, when we abandon the casino and the enclosure, we will be far from landing in a wilderness. If we start from home, we will start from the original – the primal common, which is the only true economy. As I say elsewhere, we live primarily in the household and only expediently under hierarchies. As modernity cascades around us, we need not head for the bunkers, we can reach out to family friends and neighbours. If we had previously diverted our spending from the internet and from super-markets and corporations – if we had diverted it into the shops and workshops of local trades' people, then the beginnings of a working economy of villages, towns, workshops and farms could emerge as dereliction of ring road and retail park flap like loose corrugated sheets in the similarly primal wind!

Green activists talk a lot about divestment – about diverting casino spending (central banks, pension funds, great corporations, "investors", into green spending. They shout, Oil is old, this is new. Why not grab the new coming thing? Quick before others get there first!

I say, they prolong, and for just a little, what is bleeding the true economy dry – that is enclosure. Property is deaf both to its own coming collapse and to the common, and worse, to the coming collapse of both ecosystems and climatic balance.

Many green activists talk of fighting the "big polluters", but those polluters only exist by the spending of little people. They do not exist by "big investors". It is not the supply side, which must crumble. It is the demand.

Let's shift the divestment movement to include us all. We can shed the corporate clothing by not paying for it and instead revive those same skills close to home. Close and home are both very powerful triggers of emotion. They instinctively bond.

I don't know of one academic economist who has courage to say that a steady-state, circular, or doughnut economy will cause the collapse of the casino and so by cascade, of the real economy of manufacturing, wages, tax revenue and infrastructure spending.

Ah well, here's the thing, they speak from the enclosures. What use are they on the common?

****

Of course, a junior hospital doctor has an ordinary wage. It is when she becomes a consultant, or a GP (also a consultant) that she begins to charge rent for her status. She can become rich overnight. I fully accept that for very many GPs and consultants, their vocation and not money lead them to their posts, but nevertheless their rental value remains pernicious. For our junior doctor to become a consultant (and also rich overnight), she must first publish a peer-reviewed paper, or two. It would be prudent, to focus on areas which pharmaceutical companies would find "interesting" and also to confirm the currently-fashionable status quo, rather than rocking its boat. Remember she will be horribly over-worked and under-valued and so the enticement of considerable riches and of peer respect will probably overwhelm the contrary leaning – of an innocent search for truth.

Similarly, and in many areas, the possession of a doctorate will not lead to more than an ordinary wage. It is consultancy (enclosure's gate-keeping), which does so.

For instance, in climate-related areas, researchers may be paid an ordinary wage, but "lead authors" will begin to charge status rent and can become very, very rich - and rather quickly. Commercial and government consultancy positions will, if convenient, open their doors. Any punctures appearing in their previous "research" will be attacked as schism. Respected status and sudden wealth will have been hard-fought and will not be relinquished! Humble researchers in possession of a doctorate and but a small wage, will – to keep that position and that wage – almost exclusively, back-up that "lead author".

CHAPTER 48 – LET'S BE TRAGI-COMIC

I propose that what most prevents us from evacuating both our crazy infinite-growth model and our equally crazy destruction of the natural world (which houses, clothes and feeds us) is our inability to embrace and choose the tragedies through which we must first pass to settle within Earthly means.

All roads back to Earth, must first pass through total economic collapse. We must face that, but we don't.

We create fantasies, such as net emissions, or models to slow economies, which conveniently ignore the collapse, which would ensue by their application – that is, for all growth-driven modernity.

I include ideas of green technological progress; of man-centric enlightenment; of cures for all diseases; of modernity as replacement for errors of the past; of future-created tools, which will solve current predicaments; of education as synonym for enlightenment.

The truth is, that we can only effectively apply the doughnut, or circular, or steady-state economies after collapse. Developed "economies" are now levitated so high above their terrains, that little more than a pin-prick will bring them down about our real and trembling human forms. As we wait for that collapse, we should all be busily building inter-connected homes inside the terrains, which must feed, house and clothe us. Only there, can we think of "the circular economy" and only there can we consider the common bonds that may bind communities, instead of prevalent pictures of fear, hate and bunkers. That economy must accept the rubble and ashes - the pain, unemployment, cold and hunger, which will be a part of collapse. The tragedy will come and we should embrace it now, just as we should embrace any truth. Because of that - doughnut, circular and steady-state models, begin with a lie. They refuse to evacuate the bad and to settle the good.

174

Tragedy is something artists have embraced in every century. If it exists, then we must morally-embrace it as necessary. As I say, comedy and tragedy have identical plots – so comedy is useful too. Let's be tragi-comic to keep "noble" tragedy at bay. Noble tragedy is narcissism – that silhouette on the hill-top against a wild sky – that hubris.

Pointing out the above has frozen me out from every "green" forum, which used to publish my articles – for some, because of my experience of sequestration and of my refusal to accept models, which include net emissions – for others, for my criticism of "the doughnut without collapse".

My web site has a tiny – no, smaller than tiny influence. Traffic is very, very, very small.

Ah well, that's rather comic.

****

CHAPTER 49 – A BEAUTIFUL ADVENTURE

It should be a beautiful adventure – living in community again – supplying each-others' needs. Learning the skills for that will prove to be another beautiful thing. As a tool touches its materials, so the human imagination touches the Earth. Earth reverberates at the impact. How far? Imagine all those near infinite influences touching others and creating still more sparks – some for the worse perhaps. Then, we imagine the better, like Edward Thomas paused (in his express train) at Addlestrop station – "*and for that minute a blackbird sang – and round him, mistier, further and further – all the birds of Oxfordshire and Gloucestershire.*" Would you embark from the train into that other world?

Imagine travelling again, along valleys, up gradients, crossing rivers, meeting people, sitting on a pub bench as dusk arrives and as bats replace the last swallows – both feasting on the same day's hatch – an insect feast – and all connected as the traveller is to her destination and as the intricate complexity of every species is – vibrating in both time and space from a pub bench through Oxfordshire to Gloucestershire.

Imagine the end of the internet, aviation and the family car – the end of travelling without travel and the end of google. Imagine the primary source of learning to be our senses – the sight, touch, scent and sound of the world and then also the senses (the enticing news) of others. We'd test that on our own experience, or adventure to seek it out. Thus, the tale-telling is born, which eventually mutates to stories of ancestors – commons – common mythology.

Listen – the internet, aviation, family car, suburbia... must all end anyway. They can only be powered by a consumed Earth.

It's very strange, but most people seem to want to consume the Earth, thinking the future will somehow replenish the present. They stand in a fiction – often a science fiction. Certainly, every

government of every developed economy believes in that cargo cult
– of future salvation landing from future shores on the beaches of
the present – of the Gods of Cargo. We stand on the shingle and
chant, Progress! Enlightenment! Modernity! The present is
backward. The future's the thing.

Come away, my friend, have a cup of tea and then, shall we walk a
little, on the Earth?

Let's digress –

Now, the main criticism which most green thinking aims at our
ancestor, Adam Smith is his notion of the efficiencies gained by
division of labour. We find it difficult to argue against it with
regards to efficiency, but we say, But Adam, what about the human
soul? But I think if we read Adam's thoughts as a single complex
whole, he'd have the last laugh. At the very centre of his vision is his
understanding of the evils of profit. It's true, that in all "developed"
economies, efficiencies of economies of scale have led to increased
profit, diminished wages, and diminished leisure time. He would
regard that as the deepest of cultural tragedies, which have led to
today's poverty, shrunken skill, slave labour and hoarded wealth. If
he could see us today, he would immediately note that the invisible
hand was a withered, shrunken anachronism, dangling in useless
ugliness at our sides.

> The greatest wealth of nations is seen in economies with high
> wages and low profits and the least, in economies with low
> wages and high profits.

To Adam, division of labour leads either to increases leisure time, or
to increased wages. Of course, a lovely combination might be a
smaller increase in wages knit with a smaller increase of leisure
time. How much money do we think we need? How much leisure
time do we think we need? For myself, I'd probably choose the
leisure to engage in wider economic activity – community projects
and pleasures and even occasionally, a monkish cell, or by the
peripatetic thought-stimulus of a walk by the sea-shore - to improve
the writing of this book.

Let's now consider mechanisation –

As our community settles back into its terrain, can we come
together inside a factory, so that its efficiencies generate more

leisure time? Need the fat mill-owner (Josiah Bounderby) grow fatter on the labours of his thinning slaves? Need slavery (education) be taught at a very young age, by Mr Gradgrind?

Of course, we cannot have Coketown – that is the model for what we have today - – belching unused wastes and fire-born CO_2. But we can have mills and manufactories which use the power of gravity, which, in turn, powers looms, forges, grain mills and timber working. The sluice and the water wheel are thousands of years old and can be both built and used in community. They increase leisure time, because they create goods (not necessarily for sale) in a short passage of time. People can come together there. They can sing and gossip as they work. They can weave their own designs – both practically and spiritually – function and elegance combined (Ruskin).

Profit would destroy the purpose of the mill and also increase the costs of building it. It would remove the pleasure of building it. As children, we loved to play at such designs – channelling water over, or under, or around, or into dammed pools. We'd sail stick boats and sometimes perhaps, design a water wheel. Without the need for profit and with increased leisure-time, adults can play too – inevitably leading to far simpler and better designs than our modern engineer, working within the restraints of his "brief". Remember, a resilient economy must be largely composed of money-less activity. Money is a useful tool, but no more.

I think it probable that direct traction from gravity, through water, to machinery will prove a step more efficient than gravity, through water, through turbine, through electricity to machinery.

Why not stick a very small turbine, in the sluice, for electric light, to illuminate our work in dark days?

We could do without the factory and sit in happy solitude at our cottage looms, but convivial company and more leisure time may change our minds. Remember though, profit, rent, usury and the amoral trading of the mills original source of finance – that is of tradeable shares and bonds will make the proposition irrelevant. We must abandon such monetised mills – abandon the enclosure and settle the common. Always, always, always return to the cottage and then build a community of friends. Then by common ingenuity, and on the common – build the factory. However, I think that non-

178

tradeable shares could be issued within a community for the beginnings of such adventures.

When Edward Thomas listened from his stationary express train window to those more and more distant blackbirds singing, he listened, by the chance of an interrupted journey, to an enchanting land. Let's be similarly enchanted, because our industrial journey has been well and truly interrupted – by oblivion.

****

CHAPTER 50 – LOST IN DREAMS OF ARTHUR AND GAWAIN

Yes. Our industrial journey has been interrupted by oblivion. That is simple truth. Deny it, or accept it. Of course, every government of every developed economy denies it. So, we in those economies, must quietly embark at the next station, or otherwise grab our driver; pilot; politician by the lapels and force her to stop the train. Strangely, most people prefer to stay on the train and inside their accustomed route, others would also stay on the train (most academics), but attempt to slow it down. Slightly less would stay on the train, but force it to stop, they think, by the force of powerful argument – that is the rest of academics.

Those last would remain on the stopped train but deny the human consequence of universally stopped trains – total collapse of the rail system – of wages, tax revenues, both hard and social infrastructures.

Only a very few would alight at the next station – abandoning the train for quite another sort of journey.

Those of us who alight at the next station can build a settlement without a train track to the future – to oblivion. We can live, at last in the present – like all life on Earth – responding and adapting to be one small part of the greater whole.

Meanwhile, every green NGO paces the coach corridors, raising subscriptions and persuading people to lobby their MPs to green the locomotive's energy supply and also to slow it down – sometimes they do mention that oblivion lies ahead. Yet fast, or slow, in time the train will arrive at Oblivion Station and then disappear – its insubstantial pageant faded...

Those who alight from the train are rather like the out-landers of Huxley's *Brave New World*, or E M Forster's, *The Machine Stops*. But they have a long literary and pre-literary tradition, depicted by Morris, Thoreau, Ruskin, Smith, Clare, Coleridge, Blake, Gray, Goldsmith – by the Diggers and Levellers – by Marvel, Herrick, by Milton (sort of), Shakespeare, Jonson, Sydney, Raleigh (and co), then we jump to Virgil and several others and then again to legends of the green wood and of pre-enclosure days going back deep into the Bronze Age – running counter to Tales of warrior heroes – Arthur, Cuchulainn, Hector, Achilles… All male? – Can't be helped – that's history.

Of course, most of the above remained on the train, dreaming of stepping off. You may be surprised to learn that I think the tracks were first laid in the late Bronze Age (about 1,500 BC), when "land pressures" first sprung ideas of property (enclosure) and the necessity for warrior elites to defend it.

The counter tales were of The Garden; of green-wood gods; of sacred sites – mountains, springs – the deities of the common and of ancestors.

Warrior elites are stupid – they use power, not senses. The train track is stupid. It uses power, not senses.

In the late Bronze Age, we lost the battle with stupidity and we have lost it ever since.

Today, we will lose the battle again. Fighting is pointless. As many of those writers have suggested, we leave the battlefield – turn our backs, cross the tracks and walk away – didn't our mothers always tell us that? We all know the train will run out of track and will hang, for just a moment, on empty air.

As David Jones said of his rifle, *"Leave it, leave it under the oak. Leave it for Jerry and the salvage bloke."* Though he was lost in dreams of Arthur and Gawain.

****

CHAPTER 51 – SUMPS

Now, let's return to chapter 25, *Here's Why I'm so at Odds with Many of my Green Friends*. And let's consider carbon sumps.

These are some sumps – true sumps, which it would be dangerous to unlock – coal, oil, gas, heartwood of trees, strata of layered peat (sequestered beneath the living bog), frost from the permafrost.

Of course, all have been unlocked – mostly by combustion – some by the resultant greenhouse effect and some by farmers and gardeners. In consequence we are all in extreme danger.

It is a moral tale – sumps should not leak. There we have it, that must be a simple and primal law of the commons. Commons define good and bad behaviour.

Now IPCC consider sumps to be but one part of sequestration, whereas I do not. For me, sumps and true sequestration are synonyms. IPCC consider soil life, plant and animal life to be a sequestered mass of carbon. I do not. I consider it to have mass, plus energy and velocity. It is by no means sequestered. It creates and maintains the atmosphere. It cannot be thought of as sequestered and apart from that atmosphere.

Along with coal and etc, these things are also truly sequestered – bones, limestones, phosphate rock.

Bio mass – living mass – must be considered quite differently. In the first place, it is not "carbon" – that is a static mass. In addition to mass, life has acceleration (vitality) and velocity (time, seasons, fast-growing, slow growing). Carbon cycles cannot exist without vitality – without the energy of life.

Remove energy and velocity and yes, we'd have a carbon sump, but we'd also (after a mass explosion of fermentation gases, created by the last throws of fungi and bacteria) have a dead planet.

Let's return to where I think the error might have first germinated – to James Lovelock. He is rightly revered, but his blinkered physicist's view of "carbon" was catastrophically wrong.

He saw that the sumps, which I have described, must be urgently locked-up again. But then he took another step – why not do some geo-engineering and harvest vast amounts of biomass (which he thought of as carbon) and bury it deep beneath the continuing cycles of life – removing "carbon" from the Gaia system by increasing the size of the sump. I haven't a clue why he thought that would diminish the green-house effect. I suppose he thought, undisturbed-sump – good, increased-sump – better.

Meanwhile, removing life, removes the mass, acceleration and velocity of life. It moves us closer to a lifeless planet and further from a living one. As we know, the complexity of inter-connections can lead to species cascade and still further loss of mass, energy and velocity. Remove life into a sump, or by burning it, and we diminish the power of photosynthesis to "draw down" atmospheric carbon dioxide and so we also cause the green-house to expand, as life-cycles weaken.

Ah well, whoever thought the Phoenix (living mass) could emerge from her own flames? All I can see are gas, ashes and energetic heat.

****

CHAPTER 52 – WE ARE THE CAMBIUM

Climatic catastrophes will continue to accelerate beyond all predictions, because no-one has changed the model, which produced the old predictions.

Similarly, those who remain inside the economic model, which has brought us to this moment of climatic and ecological collapse, will not prevent that collapse, or the economic collapse which must also come.

Improving the model from inside the model does not change the model. That is why the planned de-growth of the model does not change it – it merely limits its appetite. Limiting the appetite of an already fragile model will lead to implosion (starvation) and death.

We currently follow the human construction of economic and climatic models. We add to them what we think of as scientifically obtained data. That we add genuine data to a fallible model does not improve the model. What's more, it corrupts the data.

Moreover, adding genuine data to a corrupt model evokes an illusion, in the eyes of many, of a genuine model.

This is our predicament. The whole of academia, much of commerce and nearly every government of every developed economy is rigidly set on improving, de-growing and greening a model that is destined to fail. Of course, parts of commerce and governance see no need even to improve a model which provides the source of their wealth and authority.

****

Plainly, we must learn a new economic vision, which fits both the genuine data, while allowing for a far more modest human settlement.

When I say data, I mean intelligence of nature - the evidence of our senses. Science, to be science, must be sceptical – that is amoral. So, science is no help in guiding what we do. What we do as a group is the culture of that group. Scientific knowledge can advantageously add to the accumulating mythology – to the assurance and pleasures, of a culture, but scientific knowledge is not the culture. What we do is the culture – that is tools for settlement are the culture. Tools are always moral, because all actions have wider consequence. To return to my recurring metaphor, where a tool touches its material is a spark of truth, which immediately becomes a moral truth, because that touch may produce better, or worse reactions.

Thus, experiences of individuals within a culture are vital to a common settlement of its terrain, because experience is always solitary – even though it may echo the experiences of others. Shared experiences add to the binding of cultural mythology, through gossip and interest in another's skills, tools and areas of application. Where a tool (or a hand) touches its materials is the primary source for cultural (common) intelligence.

Where is governance, or rather where should it be? The oldest governance is the common – the accumulated and accumulating voices of both ancestors and ourselves. Ourselves are the current embodiment of ancestry. Thinking of the culture as a living organism, let's say, a tree - we are the cambium, but we only stand by the heartwood of ancestry. We grow around and by those ancient trunks and branches. I think many ancient cultures functioned purely in that way.

The purpose of enclosure (of property) is to remove ancestral guidance (the common) to replace it with the guidance of a hierarchy.

Religions (for the most part) have been sanctuaries for the commons, against the ephemeral and usually destructive behaviours of hierarchies. Of course, religions have often been flawed by hierarchies of their own. Nevertheless, a balance of church, temple, mosque and state has provided some protection to eroded and eroding commons.

Today, developed economies have achieved the mass enclosure of what they think of as everything, into private properties – of status,

185

money and land. Property is amoral – that is its purpose – to escape the moral judgement of the common. Enclosure's tools face no scrutiny. To obscure that obvious flaw, it creates what it hopes will prove a contagious cargo cult (sham religion) of Progress, Enlightenment, Education, for all of which, we must pay considerable rents.

Fortunately, there is also a flaw in that thought – "mass enclosure of everything" – because moral guidance – that is laws of commons – are alive and well in the household. Family, friendship and common interest groups behave by their own rules. Fair shares rule. Money and status do not. What's more, I think our lives are centred round that common. As I say, we live primarily in the household and only expediently under hierarchies.

Let's consider the opening paragraph to this chapter –

> Climatic catastrophes will continue to accelerate beyond all predictions, because no-one has changed the model, which produced the old predictions.

Plainly we must evacuate the whole thing. We must evacuate the amoral enclosures and re-settle the moral common. We shall not be stepping into a strange land, because as families and friends we are already settled there. We can begin from that heart-wood and then begin, by new relationships; by leaf and branch, to reclaim the common

To be sure, we'll enter a world of frugality; of rations; of consequence – but for palpable, immediately sensual reasons, and for the very great beauty of it all. We are the cambium – the green, photosynthetic leaves of the species.

Ah well, we cannot be photosynthetic beyond the metaphor, but nevertheless, we can grow appropriately into both our times and spaces. Let's be fitting.

****

CHAPTER 53 – IN THE OUTER LANDS

Of course, post-collapse, we'll have no choice, but to come together on the common, but what do we do now, in the last days before collapse? Plainly we can build new economic and social relationships subversively beneath the enclosures and on a rather fragile and tentative common. We can withdraw our spending from super market, retail park, the internet and so on and replace it into the hands of local trades' people. We can learn non-fossil-fuelled skills. If possible, we can evacuate the education system and begin to teach more appropriate values. Of course, the enclosures will reach down with law enforcement – compulsory curriculums, rent.

It's a muddle – for instance a renewing Earth will not have energy to power the internet, and yet for now it is useful to communicate between commoners and as a library for skills and tools. All is least worst options.

The transition movement had it right from the beginning – it has made no attempt to improve the enclosures, but rather, it would learn, step by step, to enter the common - a place where behaviour has consequence. Its footsteps lead from an economy powered by fossil fuels towards one, which isn't. It hopes for the transition community to expand across its new commons.

But still we live in a world of enclosures and we can negotiate with that world for measures, which may aid our transition, using all the allies we can get. Such measures may prove congruent with the contrary aims of others, who wish not to evacuate, but to improve the enclosures. An improved enclosure erodes the common. They include –

1. Redirecting New Deal, or Green New Deal moneys from corporate re-finance, to community re-finance – from corporate greening to community greening. We can use it to help settle the common.

2. Basic Income, or Citizen's dividend is seen by many as the best way to rejuvenate existing "economies" during and as we emerge from the Coronavirus "slow down".

It can be similarly used to buy liberty to settle the common. Tom Paine saw it as a means to some restorative justice, by returning the rents gathered by enclosure, back to the original common. Of course, it remains a small restoration – that is, merely for rents gathered. Meanwhile, the theft of moral commons to create amoral private property is the cause not only of most poverty in the world, but also of climatic disbalance and of the pillage of nature. Its course is inevitable – self-destruction. Truly, we must evacuate quick. Enclosures cannot be improved. Self-destruction is intrinsic to what they are. Those who'd enclose, can have no moral understanding to respond to moral advice.

"Carbon" taxes can be used in the same way – to re-finance community endeavour – through citizen's dividend perhaps. Those who'd "improve" the enclosures (most environmental activists) could also be helpful to those who, on the contrary, would re-settle the common. The "great corporations", for the most part, will be happy to embrace carbon taxes, because they know coal, oil and gas are bad for sales figures, whereas consumer trends are towards an "enlightened" future of green energy. Progress, enlightenment and new green technologies are excellent marketing tools for continued and utterly amoral (and so immoral) "green" enclosure. Corporations will be keen to swallow as much Green New Deal and Carbon Tax money as they can. The negotiated battle between community and corporate funding is on-going inside the enclosures. In the end it remains a part of this illusion – consumerism as a partnership. Corporations need the consumer and most consumers need the corporation. I think that is an unhappy relationship. I think most people are unhappy. Retail therapy is becoming less and less effective.

The common is a still, small voice. It sings and dances – inviting others to the dance. I wish I knew if and when it will become more insistent. Time is very, very short.

****

CHAPTER 54 – I SAID I'D NOT SPEAK OF VIRUSES, BUT I'VE CHANGED MY MIND

People are shocked by the Tory government's behaviour during Coronavirus, when it had been elected to do exactly what it is doing. I cannot fathom why people are shocked, since it was our choice and also the choice of the BBC and the bulk of other media organisations (including the Guardian). It promised deregulation, privatisation, decreased taxation for the rich and increased burdens for the poor. It promised a firm hand to repel and persecute black and brown people, an easing of police regulation (though no increased funding). It promised increased limits to liberty to both protest and hold public gatherings. It promised to limit democratic governance and to increase powers of arrest. Many of those powers were promised to private mercenary and "security" firms, who were also offered the management of prisons. It promised to privatise education, probation services and many other services besides. It promised to accelerate the slashing of environmental and human rights legislation and thus also to increase the power of private enterprise.

It promised (by plain implication, not text) to hand both medical supplies and treatments (pharmaceuticals, vaccines...) to the patent-spurred "ingenuity" of private enterprise. Similarly, by implication, it promised profit to that private enterprise by allowing private patents for work done by public taxation – thus further reducing accountable infrastructure.

It proposed to enclose tax-generated and so common infrastructures into private properties – without the acts of parliament formerly necessary for all such enclosures.

Why does the Left affect outrage at what it had itself achieved by the fictional demonisation of Jeremy Corbyn? Without the liberal Left; without the Guardian newspaper, Mr Corbyn would now, by normal democratic process, be prime minister. That is no conspiracy theory, it is simple truth.

Of course, much of the above will be maintained by Mr Keir Starmer. The Liberal Left chose him, because it also chose corporate-supplied consumerism, which is exactly what we have now. It chose a more policed, yet diminished state. It chose what it now rails against – that is, a politicised virus. Coronavirus has been politicised to open the UK door to stateless, private spoils of war. Yet the virus is promoted as an enemy to be defeated by a united nation – a little and glorious England (forgetting N Ireland, Scotland and Wales), which against overwhelming odds and by the universal self- sacrifice of her people, will eventually, scarred, limping, but unwavering, emerge victorious from the trenches.

That the virus is just a virus and that species can neither function, nor evolve without viruses, is brushed behind the door by both the "stick to the patent-extraction of the science" of the liberal left and the battlefield – the survival of the "fittest" - of the extreme right.

Don't forget – no never forget, that the Third Reich was financed, enabled and industrialised (contrary to its ideals) entirely by private enterprise, which throughout the terror, continued to extract large profits from both the Reich and from those increasing spoils of war.

Wars will always make a few very rich indeed.

Listen! There is no war. There are collapsing ecologies and there is a wildly disbalancing climate. Look after your family, friends and neighbours, protect the vulnerable, but turn away from the illusion of a battlefield. Neither is the ecological and climatic crisis an alternative battlefield. We are not under attack. We are receiving the effects of our own causes. The real battlefield is private, personal and epic. It is with ourselves. Please engage. Study ourselves, and we may find answers to many questions.

****

CHAPTER 54 – DRAWING TO A CLOSE

I think that this little piece of writing is drawing to a close. I think the journeys of Home sapiens are drawing to a close. All human endeavour is drawing to a close. It had stepped beyond the limits of its home on Earth and is now standing on empty air. About a quarter of the species is so cemented to its achievements that it cannot turn back. The other three quarters, who remain on the remains of a pillaged Earth have no voice to carry to those who stand in empty air. Earth's living systems are unravelling into lifelessness and the end is not far. *

For this writer, he can muddle along by the power of imagination – of the utopias that are certainly possible, but which he knows are extremely unlikely. He can survive by the tragic comedy of it all. But sometimes good music will pluck inner strings, beyond words and have him collapsed in a sobbing heap on the floor.

Cultures, as he repeats like a mantra, are what people do - not what they have achieved, or possess. So, culturing is always in the timeless present – it is being in the sensual union of ourselves and our terrains. So also, we can only change the course of a culture in that sensual moment. It can never be deferred into a targeted future. Only my present can contribute to the larger future

A climate activist's contribution to a common future is not words delivered from a podium, but her share of the jet aeroplane, which delivered her to the conference.

Her understanding of the data she presents to assembled delegates should have made it impossible for her to board the aeroplane. That it hasn't, indicates nothing more than the power of what she thinks of as her power and perhaps - of a longing to "belong" among her peers. That she reads from a document, which could have been published for all to see without stirring from home, is both tragic and comic – perfect for black comedy and for the most-stark of

Greek tragedies. At the time, her present contributed only to a rosy future for jet aeroplanes.

That's all I have to say.

We can choose to step back from those targeted futures and into our lives and their real effects. I don't think we will, but we could.

That "we could" is all that keeps this writer grasping the shimmering beauty of a fragile spider's thread.

****

* *It is the power of spending, not the size of population, which has pillaged the Earth.*

THE END

APPENDAGE

This book has ended, but the following (written in May 2019) has a little biography within it. Otherwise, it was a sort of precursor to the book and is not essential reading.

My world is very small. I've not travelled much and not at all beyond Welsh, Scots, Irish and English shores. Yet, I think the parish of Llannefydd, where I've lived and worked since 1975, provides an accurate-enough microcosm of anywhere that has not been recently ravaged by war, invasion, empire, flood, drought and famine. Earlier, as a teenager in suburban Woking, I devoured books of all sorts, absorbing the knowledge and insights of revered authorities and resting in what I thought was their beauty and truth. I decided then, in the 1960s that oil and its ways of life were destructive and I also vowed never to fly – and I never have and never will. I suppose John Ruskin, William Morris, On Walden Pond and so on, led me to that conclusion. I was what is now called a school phobic. I have no education. That has been a valuable asset to finding my way. Everywhere, I see education's distorted and blinkered perspective – particularly, of course in people of influence, because I must repel that influence. A friend has written that he and I are the Shakespeare-quoting outlanders of Huxley's Brave New World. Would I still love Shakespeare and Chaucer, had I an education? – I doubt it.

I hope this is not a narcissistic journey. I remain uneasily in the first person, because I've stumbled into a need to explore why I think and feel as I do. I focus on myself, because what I think and feel is mine (my fault) and not that of the "we" of family, friends and influences.

Having escaped suburbia, I spent five years working on archaeological digs, until I fell into farming by accident. Now in my mid-twenties, I spent a winter at leisure (on accumulated wages) in a very beautiful place and when I eventually ran out of money, found that I did not want to leave. Farm labouring was the only local work and I came to enjoy it. Soon, I began to rent some nearby fields. It was very much easier for me than it is for today's young people. In 1976, a friend and neighbour, simply and trustingly, bought me twenty-three ewes – selected with the skilled advice of another friend and neighbour. With that first lamb crop, I repaid the money in the first year. That also, could not happen today. It could not have happened then, without the kindliness, trust, time, money and wisdom of neighbours – most of whom were born and hefted into that cynefin. They displayed the timeless common of such communities – hospitality to and curiosity for strangers. Meanwhile, because I continued to work for five days a week as a farm labourer and so needed no other maintenance, the ewes soon increased to three hundred. This is not a story of hard graft and steely determination rewarded – not at all - I enjoyed regular music nights in the local pub and partying generally. Tragically, for anyone today, it would have to be hard graft and steely determination and even then, it would probably end in failure.

It was a world of unspoken commons, untouched by NGO, government, corporation, or bank. Although that world has almost gone, it does remain in us all, as a kind of folk memory and I speculate that there are few who'd not long for its revival if they just let the emotion to rise. Most commons have been enclosed - by consumer rights, consumer dependency and by monopolies of supply, information and the ballot. However, I think the common does survive in the ethics of the household; in filial codes and memories. Once upon a time, many aspects of the commons were preserved in church, chapel, mosque, temple... Even though the power of religious institutions led to the very human problems of all power structures, nevertheless those institutions often stood as foils to many forms of enclosure – latterly, at least of ethics.

Of course, under the wing of Protestantism (Protestantism herself was not guilty), older commons of both land-use and the trades were swept away – mutating into fabulous wealth for aristocrats and larger yeoman farmers and into new slums, starvation and prostitution for the migrating dispossessed. Power's excuse was a conveniently-adopted religion. We can see a similarity today, as the powers put on a fervent green mantle, as a means to the coming new money-spinner – claiming both virtue (as in the Reformation) and a new source of enclosed and fabulous wealth. As the old sources (oil) slip away, the opportunistic see that "renewable" energy must be exploited and enclosed - Monopolies get used to monopoly. How marvellous that a new money-spinner can wear a cloak of green virtue, just as the vicious enclosures of the sixteenth century Reformation wore a cloak of religious virtue.

What are commons? I say they are the long-evolved (and evolving) moral guidance of the similarly long experience of ancestors. Those morals survive, embodied in the living, at many levels from shallow to deep. They urge what must be done to conserve both the culture and the species – including species on which ours depend. They overrule ephemeral coercions of power. Often, they define the roles of power. At the deepest level they emerge in the intrinsic morals, which we think (or rather, feel) make us human. We have the muscular form of who we are, but also the moral form of what we do. Taboo belongs in that realm. I think enlightenment is wrong to sneer at taboo. Meanwhile, at the shallowest level (though tinged with the deep) commons emerge in rights to land and water responsibility, to pannage, estovers, pasture, piscary, flotsam and so on. All commons define rights to responsibility. They outline both rations of what we can have and a ration of what we can do. Don't forget that the true home of economics is moral philosophy. It is also the household itself. If we understand household budgets and household rules of behaviour then we know all we need to know of economies generally. Casino "economists" will disagree.

Commons define behaviour. Present cultural behaviour germinates the cultural future. The future cannot undo what the present has done. That is a potent thought. Enclosure – property – only concerns nouns. It is a fence line for irresponsible protection of time-freed nouns (the liberal economy) and for the exclusion of unruly verbs – that is, the effects of causes, including the guidance of moral philosophers and real economists.

Because they've evolved to do so, children quickly learn the subtlety of commons. Often, commons involve rituals of initiation and coming of age, in which we put on the spirit of passed ancestors - to live in the same bequeathed and rationed space. We curate our inheritance as we can and then bequeath it in turn.

Enclosure defines right to irresponsibility – to private property with which I can behave as I choose. All enclosures are the same – of land, money, ideas and status. They remove both lessons of history and needs of the future. That is the state we are in today – total enclosure of the last social commons, with no past and no future. Land-owners can pillage as they choose - money owners likewise. GP; solicitor; consultant; "professional" people, extract terrible rents (that is riches) from communities they once served and to maintain the ways of life, (the class system) to which they've grown accustomed. Their monopoly cannot be challenged by other than their own professional bodies – peer review has become a mutually supportive career ladder. In theory at least, peer review once provided useful insights to those with open minds, but today it serves only to increase the barbs of the fence-line, which excludes schismatic "peers" who'd rock an established and lucrative boat. And so it is that my simple mind has no trust for scientific papers – even though it is curious for the science. To those who ask for a list of sources beneath my articles, I say Pshaw! The source is mine. If we cannot think for ourselves, why burden the world with more clutter? A paraded dignity of peers cannot increase the dignity of my words – they are what they are for themselves... Of course, I'd attribute quotations and influences.

Anyway, it came to pass, as proper stories say, that I met a farmer's daughter and married into a small farm. In 1987 we decided to register the farm with the Soil Association for organic conversion.

My rented hill land had been organically managed since 1978, but we now had the pleasure of arable crops and eventually an orchard and veg field. Eventually too, we managed to escape the commodity market and sell much of our produce over market stalls as food – not commodity - to real people, face to face – that is, all our vegetables, apples, apple juice, beef and lamb. We sold only what we grew on the farm. For the future, we must do the same for cereals and pulses.

Here is this season's picture of our small, organically-managed farm – 66 acres of marginal to good land (grade three) and a further 23 acres of rented hill land, which is unsuitable for cropping – The 66 acres breaks down as 10 acres of an oats/barley/pea mix and 7 acres of oats – all for combining, plus 2 acres of apples and 3 acres of vegetables. The bulk of the energy required for the 5 acres of apples and vegetables is manual. Whereas, the 17 acres for combining is almost entirely diesel powered. The remaining 44 acres provides minimal woodland, being mostly grassland. It is diesel powered for hay and silage, but mostly "dog and stick" for the rest. Is that sustainable? For the apples, vegetables and dog and stick – If very well managed, possibly. For the rest – No.

The rented 23 acres of hill land, includes about an acre of grazed oak woodland. Our (entirely benign) landlord has retained about 4 acres of oak woodland which is a part of the whole - but our part is pasture and mostly by dog and stick. Is that sustainable? No. Such land would be more beneficial as woodland – economically, ecologically and photo-synthetically.

I reckon a rule of thumb for crop rotation is one year of extractive crops to two years of regenerative green manure or pasture. (we practice 2 years cereal to 4 years grass/clover) I think there is little to choose between green manure, or grazing – both are effective. Yes, I do think we could have a vegan agriculture. However, grazing has two advantage – One – it removes the considerable energy required (human, or diesel) to cut and mulch. Two – it provides useful eggs, milk, butter, cheese and meat to the community. There is a plausible third advantage – a balance of plant to animal, could replicate the proportions of that balance in nature. Nature has evolved for optimum success. So! – introducing animals into a rotation may achieve optimum agricultural success. Of course, for the future, our meat ration will not stretch to every day, but only to weekends and special occasions. Cereals and pulses must feed people. We'll have none to spare for batteries, broiler houses and feed-lots.

So, at Bryn Cocyn, the 20 acres of arable and vegetable cropping, need 40 acres of green manure/pasture to maintain their fertility – leaving only 6 acres, of which 2 are woodland and 2 are apples. That means we must plant a further 2 acres with trees. We are about to do so. However, what of those 23 acres of hill land, which cannot support cropping? I think they should be returned to their natural state – that is woodland. We haven't done so. I am guilty. Because we easily sell all our lamb and beef by market stalls, providing a large part of our income, my economy has trumped my ecology, stepping beyond its sustainable ration. It is no dispensation that

197

most UK farms are far, far worse. My excuse? – We are step-by-step in transition.

In Wales, we export 80% of the lamb we produce, which makes for an obviously precarious future. If we thought of 80% of sheep-producing land, repurposed as new woodland, then we could also think of both a more stable economy and a more stable ecology. In addition, we'd add considerably to Welsh photosynthetic power. I don't like the word, sequestration – it implies a still and quiet mass. It also leads to wrong thinking. The truth is that life in soil, bacteria, fungi, plant and animal is dynamic, fluid, inter-changeable and vivacious! Those who use the term to describe an accumulated mass of carbon (such as IPCC & most of the climate glitterati) are deluded. Climate glitterati? I borrow the term from Kevin Anderson.

In short, I think we need cropping land to grow food and unless two thirds if it is dairy/meat-producing ley pasture, only a third of that area can actually produce food for people. I think all other land should grow trees. Readers must know that I don't share the wild sequestration claims of the "pasture-fed" evangelists. Neither do I share the polemical yield statistics by those such as George Monbiot, who attribute to vegetable yield, three times its true yield – by ignoring the regenerative phases of rotation – and by similarly diminishing animal yield, by dismissing its integrated part in that rotation. Animals (as in nature) add to, rather than diminish the whole. George is polemical for the animal part of re-wilding. Why should he not be so for the increased biomass (yield) achieved by the grazing of green manures in vegetable/cereal/pulse rotation? I like George's rewilding ideas (although we shall need timber for construction), but he is lazy and conveniently selective when he comes to food production. Even so, I agree with George that fields dedicated purely to animal production are a waste of space (I am guilty). What's more, those fields for the most part (unless Bronze/Iron Age field systems) are not "traditional", they are a legacy of the brutal clearances of people from the land to allow for the golden fleece. Wool made aristocrats fabulously rich. As Thomas More accurately said, Sheep have devoured the people. Now, although it shouldn't be, wool is worthless and sheep meat income is purely subsidy. We've an acute shortage of timber and forestry (per acre) provides far, far more employment than beef and sheep production.

We let our hedges grow untrimmed – I'd say they are about fifteen feet tall on average – with blossom in the spring and nuts and berries in autumn. Most new agroforestry schemes in large-field arable land have no more "forest" than we have with small fields and wide traditional hedges. From Bryn Cocyn we can look East across the Vale of Clwyd to the Clwydian Range beyond and we can scan from Prestatyn and Rhyl in the North to Llangollen in the South. That vast area is a desert of neat and tightly trimmed hedges. No wonder it has become routine for our neighbours to spray for aphids. What if all those thousands of farms let hedges escape to the sky? It would provide the most rapid ecological and photosynthetic benefit I can imagine. We have an 8.5 acre and a 9.5 acre field, which I'd love to divide with new hedges, to make all the fields in Bryn Cocyn between 3 and 5 acres – good for organising both arable and grazing rotations.

Anyway, to assist our step-by-step transition, five years ago, I cashed in my small pension and bought a 6kw wind turbine. We also have 4kw of older solar panels and 3kw for my son's new house. We don't borrow money and we've not accumulated enough for electric vehicles.

Because my world is small, small influences to the wider world can remain large to me and also serve as a paradigm for the far larger influences which they have reflected.

The following is very close to me and my small world. I believe it to be a shrunken replica of most citizens, large NGOs and the larger world. Around 1990 or so, a charismatic, ambitious and rather narcissistic group rose to steer the course of the Soil Association. They saw their task as pushing "organic" into the mainstream. They wanted organic products in super markets, large restaurant chains and in "mainstream" thinking. They focused on this alone - the larger the organic market, so the greater the beneficial organic acreage to supply it. They adopted the necessary code phrases – such as paradigm shift, green-sky thinking...- while also creating the necessary human-sized imagery - community supported agriculture, box schemes... Neither of those had power to dilute their vision (as they should have done) rather, they lent the Soil Association false credence.

The annual Soil Association conference, became not a place where delegates from the shires assembled and shared news, knowledge and concerns, but an outright political rally, in which those charismatic leaders and panels of invited "celebrities" took (pre-submitted) questions from the floor. Those celebrities would know nothing of organic techniques, but would convey the illusion to attendees that they had entered a world of serious "movers and shakers". At one conference, Vandana Shiva spoke eloquently of lost commons and the fight to reclaim them. Like Greta Thunberg, she is a powerful speaker and I, most of the floor and the charismatic leaders were left with tears in our eyes. Yet one by one, having listened to Vandana, each charismatic leader, addressed the rest of us with the same message – that the world is as it is – that super markets are here to stay – that we'd better get real about enclosures - that we'd better goddam get on the Titanic, because the rest of the world was going nowhere.

Of course, that was my last conference. I failed utterly to influence that NGO and yet I remain a member – hoping against hope to revive its original commons.

Those who'd electrify the Titanic, can't see that the problem is the Titanic. Those who'd green their wealth can't see that the problem is wealth. Those who'd green the super market can't see that the problem is the super market. Those who'd green the enclosures (by a green new deal perhaps), can't see that the problem is the enclosures…. They can't see that to be effective, a green new deal must enter the common.

For renewable energy to stand inside terrestrial limits, it can only service the rationed limits of good behaviour. It has not capacity to service bad behaviour. Wind turbines and solar panels face terrestrial rations of mass, acceleration – space and time. I speculate that we can gratefully accept their energy for domestic heat, light, refrigeration and cookery, but no more. For transport, we must return to the world we had before fossil fuels. We must abandon suburbia, centralised procurement/distribution, all aviation, the family car… Why not? We can have sail trade, vivid and vivacious villages and towns, canals and navigable rivers. We can have a re-centred suburbia, interspersed with market gardens and dairies … We can have lively coastal towns and villages – their harbours re-built along every mile of coastline, for small-boat fishing and both

200

shore-hopping and open-sea trades. We can have full employment. We'll have plenty of now-idle metal work and so on for re-purposing. We will have acceleration due to people and not acceleration due to oil. What's more two people working side by side are more or less equal, until one gains an oil engine, car, aeroplane ticket, large high-consumption house... Money flow must shrink from acceleration due to fossil fuels to acceleration due to people – the energy of people - the power of what people can do. Why does no-one speak of acceleration? Why in carbon calculations does no-one enter the energy in living biomass – that is the power, not merely the mass of life? They (IPCC and most others) enter nouns, but not verbs. Anyway, GDP (spending) must shrink to at least a tenth (probably more) of what it is today (UK). It must shrink from fossil mass to biomass. That fossil mass was expendable, being converted into both energy and a mass of atmospheric $CO.2$ and other gases. However, biomass must remain as biomass to live breathe, photosynthesise, die and recycle. – only its intrinsic energy, including human energy (converted from food-mass) can be thought of as energy. Our lives cannot transcend the cycles of all the other lives. We must learn (or re-learn) to join those cycles to find optimum cultural success.

GDP may be a useful measure of money exchange, but it is a ridiculous measure of an economy. Ebbs and flows of the market are the concerns of a casino. Casinos wreck economies. My readers will know that the economic destruction of war, natural disasters and so on, increases GDP, even though, in the process, cultural assets have been considerably shrunk. Of course, for much that maintains economies, no money passes hands – the activities of households, parenthood, fairs and festivals – we can list many things. Economies are maintained by agreed commons of good behaviour – the good life as it learns to fit its rations of space and time.

Have Greta Thunberg and the Extinction Rebellion been manufactured, just as the organic movement has been manufactured?

1. **Yes.** I've no doubt that Cory Morningstar's research is largely accurate.
   http://www.feasta.org/2019/05/06/greta-thunberg-pr-and-the-climate-emergency/

2. **No.** I've no doubt that Greta is Greta – flesh and blood and heart and soul. I've no doubt that most who swell the Extinction Rebellion are so likewise. I've also no doubt that there are some members of the Soil Association, who still dream of lost organic commons – vivacious towns and villages, re-centred suburbia and a renaissance of the skills of the trades – accompanied of course by the decay of oil-powered super market, large food manufacturers, restaurant chains and out of, or edge of town retail/industrial parks.

3. **Yes.** How else could the school strikes and the extinction gatherings have reached all forms of media so fast without shady manipulation? How else could Greta, so swiftly address the UN, parliaments various, assembled Hollywood super-stars, or be photographed with jet-setting Naomi Klein, Al Gore and so on...?

4. **No.** The imaginations of many have been fired by both movements – not by the manipulators, but by the movements themselves.

So, we could put the problem like this – Have the movements been enclosed? I'd say both yes and no. Both are sufficiently on the common to entirely reclaim their commons. Yet both are sufficiently in an enclosure to be in very real danger of total manufacture and manipulation.

I say, Viva school strikes and extinction rebellions! But I also say, where are you going and what do you mean? I say, governments and corporations have not caused species extinction, or climatic instability. Governments and corporations have assisted we little people to behave badly, but because governments and corporations are merely ideas, the physical causes are entirely ours. Our rebellion should be against ourselves. We can step out of enclosure and onto a personal moral common. Government manipulation has assisted the rich to become richer and so the poor to become poorer – so is that where the true government-against-people battleground lies? – an inequity emergency? We can say that ecological destruction and climatic imbalance are largely caused by the rich – that the poor have not the spending power. That's true, but even if justice was done and we were re-empowered, we'd still need a clear picture of where we were going and of right and wrong behaviour.

It's plain from the above that my own life has some small successes, but also a large portion of failure. I know this – I cause climate change. I contribute to ecological catastrophe. How much? Forget that. All I know is that I must contribute less to destruction and more to a durable way of living. Collectively, we are at a point, where every road we choose will be through a variety of differing tragedies. We cannot avoid tragedy. Nemesis was our consumer-choice. Listen – literature, theatre, music, painting... can make tragedy both beautiful and true – so can a good life. For any future at all, the casino (which most call an economy) must collapse, or be collapsed about our ears. It will be highly unpleasant. I leave that to your imagination. Our task is to begin to construct an economy and a culture which is disconnected from the casino - one that can emerge more or less alive - tragic comic - conversing and loving - laughing and crying – beautiful and true - from beneath the rubble. Greening our current way of life will be suicide.

The common is a realm of rationing, maintenance, knowledge and celebration. Scattered here and there, some cultures still practice those things – people call them indigenous cultures – I've not fathomed why.

All cultures are indigenous. It's urgent to discover both how and why. Then we must come to see that cultures are not what we have, or have achieved. They are what we do.

****